مهارتها

چگونه با یادگیری تکنیکها، دانشجو و زبان آموز بهتری باشیم

دکتر آزاده نعمتی

Copyright © 2014 Dr. Azadeh Nemati
All rights reserved.
ISBN: 6006410052
ISBN-13: 978-6006410050

دعای مطالعه

خداوندا مرا از تاریکی نادانی نجات ده و به من نورانیت دانایی کرامت فرما.

خدایا برما درهای رحمتت را بگشا و گنجینه های علوم و دانشت را بگستران.

به لطف ورحمتت، ای مهربانترین مهربانان .

فهرست

مقدمه	1
تکنیکهای مطالعه	3
مکان مطالعه	4
روش مطالعه	4
دوره کردن	5
یادداشت برداری	7
تکنیکهای تمرکز	9
تکنیکهایی برای حافظه بهتر و فراموشی کمتر	10
نمودار فراموشی ابینگهایس (Ebbinghaus)	11
تکنیکهای امتحان	13
اضطراب امتحان	13
مقیاس اضطراب امتحان ساراسون	13
تکنیکهای استفاده از دیکشنری	17
دیکشنری به ما چه می آموزد؟	17
تکنیک یادگیری لغات	22
پر بسامد ترین کلمات	27
تکنیکهای خواندن	28
تکنیکهای نوشتن	35
تکنیکهای صحبت کردن و گوش دادن	37
منابع انگلیسی	38
1,000 Most Frequently Used Words	39
2,000 Most Frequently Used Words	51
The Academic Word List	69

مقدمه

یکی از مهمترین مهارتهای یادگیری ، مهارت خواندن یا چگونگی مطالعه کتابها است. اغلب به دانش آموزان و دانشجویان گفته می شود که خوب درس بخوانند، اما راه های خوب درس خواندن به آنها آموزش داده نمی شود. همه دوست دارند که سریعتر بخوانند و بیشتر و بهتر متوجه شوند. اما چگونه می توان به این اهداف دست یافت؟

دنیای امروز دنیای تغییر و تحول است . براساس آمارهای به دست آمده 56٪ از شغل های مختلفی که در سال 2005 وجود داشت اکنون وجود ندارد و این بدان معناست که تغییر و تحول در آینده نیز بسیار زیاد خواهد بود. به همین خاطر دوران فراگیری و آموزش در مقاطع مختلف تحصیلی و دانشگاهی فرصت مناسبی است که افراد مهارت های بسیاری را کسب نمایند. این مهارت ها می تواند شامل: مهارت خواندن، تحقیق کردن و درک بالاتر از متون مختلف باشد .

این کتاب شامل تدریس مهارت های مختلفی است که اولین مهارت آن مهارت مطالعه و یادگیری است.

مهارت مطالعه می تواند پایه و اساس مهارت های دیگر باشد. به همین دلیل در بخش اول مهارت مطالعه توضیح داده خواهد شد و بخش دوم به تدریس مهارتهایی اختصاص دارد که برای یادگیری زبان انگلیسی و شرکت در آزمونهای تافل (TOEFL) و آیلتس (IELTS) مناسب است.

قبل از آنکه به آموزش مهارتهای مختلف برای یادگیری زبان و آمادگی درآزمونهای تافل و آیلتس پرداخته شود، بررسی انواع مختلف آزمونهای تافل لازم است.

با نگاهی به جدول زیر مشخص می شود که در هر نوع آزمون تافل چه مهارتی سنجیده می شود.

Internet-based TOEFL	Paper-based TOEFL	Computer-based TOEFL
Listening	Listening	Listening
Speaking	Structure	Structure
Ready	Reading	Reading
writing	Test of written English	writing

در جدول بالا نشان داده شده است که قبلاً درآزمون تافل قسمت structure یا گرامر جداگانه سنجیده می شد اما اکنون و در internet based TOEFL گرامر امتحان جداگانه ای ندارد و با ارزیابی مهارتهای دیگر گرامر نیز سنجیده می شود.

قبل از شروع آموزش مهارتها لازم است در نظر گرفته شود که هر دانشجو با دانشجوی دیگر متفاوت است ولی این تفاوت ها به این معنی نیست که کسی برتر یا پایین تر از شخص دیگری است. اگر شما با نقاط مثبت و منفی خود بیشتر آشنا شوید می توانید به خودتان کمک کنید. پس در گام اول به سوالات زیر صادقانه پاسخ دهید .

پرسشنامه علاقه

1. دوست دارید در ساعات استراحت، چه کاری انجام دهید؟
2. به چه درس هایی علاقه دارید؟
3. چه درس هایی را دوست ندارید؟
4. فرض کنید در یک روز هیچ کاری برای انجام دادن ندارید، در این صورت به چه کاری می پردازید؟
5. اگر قرار باشد شخص مهمی در دنیا باشید، دوست دارید چه کسی باشید؟
6. عنوان بهترین کتابی که خوانده اید چه بوده است؟
7. به چه کتابهایی بیشتر علاقه دارید؟
8. آیا در سال گذشته کتابی را برای تفریح خوانده اید؟ نام آن را بنویسید؟
9. آیا هر روز روزنامه می خوانید؟ اگر جوابتان مثبت است چه روزنامه ای و چه قسمتی از آن را می خوانید؟
10. آیا به خواندن کتاب های کمدی علاقه دارید؟ اگر بله، چه کتابی؟
11. برنامه های تلویزیونی مورد علاقه شما چیست؟
12. آیا غالباً کتاب می خوانید یا گاهی، یا اصلاً کتاب نمی خوانید؟
13. آیا عضو کتابخانه هستید؟ هر از چندگاهی از کتابخانه استفاده می کنید؟ اغلب ، گاهی یا هرگز؟
14. چگونه این کلاس می تواند علاقه شما را نسبت به مطالعه افزایش دهد؟

اکنون می توانید جدول زیر را برای تمام دروس دانشگاهی به کار برید.

نام درس	نام استاد	ساعت	درجه سختی یا آسانی درس از نظر شما

1= سخترین 2= کمی سخت 3 = آسان 4= کمی آسان 5= ساده ترین

تکنیکهای مطالعه

تکنیک های مطالعه

اغلب گمان می رود که در سطح دانشگاه دیگر نیازی به تدریس مهارت های مطالعه نیست. شاید شما بعضی از همکلاسی های خود را دیده اید که با کمترین زمان مطالعه بیشترین نمره را کسب کرده اند و حتماً پیش خود فکر کرده اید که چرا ؟
مهارت مطالعه فقط به مطالعه زبان انگلیسی مربوط نمی شود. یادگیری این مهارت ها برای تمامی دروس لازم است.
در این فصل با مهارت های مطالعه آشنا می شوید. از این پس می توانید از این مهارت ها برای خواندن تمامی دروس استفاده نمایید و در پایان نتیجه بهتری کسب کنید.
قبل از اینکه به مطالعه هر کتابی بپردازید نکات زیر را در نظر داشته باشید.
یاد بگیرید چگونه کتاب جدید را مرور کنید .
قبل از مطالعه هر کتابی باید آن را مرور کنید . این کار را باید برای تمامی کتابهایی که توسط استادان برای درس های مختلف ارائه می شود انجام داد.
اکنون یکی از کتابهای درسی معرفی شده توسط اساتید را بردارید و به سوالات زیر پاسخ دهید .

1. نام کتاب چیست؟
2. نام نویسنده یا نویسندگان را بنویسید؟
3. تاریخ انتشار کتاب را بنویسید؟
4. مقدمه آن را بخوانید و آن را خلاصه کنید؟

5. فهرست کتاب را بخوانید . کتاب دارای چند فصل می باشد؟ کتاب چند صفحه دارد؟ نام فصلها را بنویسید؟
6. کتاب را ورق بزنید آیا در آن تصویر، جدول، نقشه، وجود دارد؟ آیا در آخر هر فصل سوالاتی پرسیده شده است؟
7. سختی یا آسانی کتاب را ارزیابی کنید، آیا خواندن این کتاب برای شما سخت است؟
8. به آخر کتاب توجه کنید آیا ضمیمه یا واژه نامه ای وجود دارد؟
9. پاسخ به سوالات بالا مرور کتاب شما را می سازد و می تواند در آینده به شما کمک کند؟

اینکه کتاب در چه سالی چاپ شده و چاپ چندم است و یا روش کار کتاب چگونه است؟ پاسخ به این سوالات می تواند در یادگیری مطالب به شما کمک کند. اگر کتاب برای شما سخت است نشان می دهد برای مطالعه کتاب به تلاش بیشتری نیاز دارید.

مکان مطالعه

نگاهی به مکان مطالعه خود بیاندازید. کجا مطالعه می کنید و چگونه تمرکز می کنید؟ شاید تعجب کنید که مکان مطالعه می تواند بر روی میزان تمرکز شما اثر بگذارد. چند دقیقه فکر کنید مطالعه شما چگونه است و در جدول زیر موارد و شرایطی که باعث به هم زدن تمرکز شما می شود را بنویسید.

راه هایی که می توانم آن را برطرف کنم	شرایطی که تمرکز را برای من مشکل می سازد
1	1
2	2
3	3

روش مطالعه

یکی از بهترین راهها برای پیشرفت مهارت مطالعه یافتن روشی برای درس خواندن است. ممکن است تاکنون روش مناسبی برای مطالعه پیدا کرده باشید. ولی اگر هنوز روش مناسبی را پیدا نکرده اید این روش را که به عنوان روش SQ3R مشهور است به کار برید. زیرا همانطور که می دانید خواندن تنها، برای یادگیری کافی نیست و بدین معنا نیست که شما مطمئناً تمام مطالب را آموخته اید.

روش SQ3R یک تکنیک جالب برای یادگیری مطالب است، روش این تکنیک به صورت زیر است.

S	Q	3 R
u	u	Read
r	e	Recite
v	s	Review
e	t	
y	i	
	o	
	n	

در روش بالا:

S=Survey یعنی قبل از مطالعه نظری اجمالی به مطالب بیاندازید. به عبارت دیگر قبل از شروع مطالعه کارهای زیر را انجام دهید.

1- به عنوان دقت کنید.
2- اولین پاراگراف را بخوانید.
3- اولین جمله از هر پاراگراف را بخوانید.
4- پاراگراف آخر یا نتیجه را بخوانید.

Q=question قبل از خواندن پاراگرافها و متن از خودتان سوالاتی بپرسید که جواب آن مربوط به مطالب مربوطه باشد.

R=Read حالا مطالب را بخوانید.

R=Recite و در قدم بعد جواب سوالها را دوباره تکرار کنید.

R=Review و سپس مطالب جمع آوری شده را مرور کنید. روش صحیح دوره کردن در قسمت بعد توضیح داده شده است.

دوره کردن

الف) مدل چرخشی آکسفورد(Oxford)

براساس مدل چرخشی آکسفورد (1990) دانشجویان باید کلمات را یا هر مطلب خوانده شده ای را دوره کنند. اولین قسمت دوره کردن باید بلافاصله بعد از تمام شدن مطالب باشد زیرا همانطور که بعدا اشاره خواهد شد پس از 20 دقیقه 80٪ مطالب از یاد می روند. پس حداکثر 20 دقیقه بعد باید تمام کلمات یا هر درس جدیدی دوباره مطالعه شود و دوباره بعد از 3 ساعت، بعد از 1 روز- 2 روز- 4 روز- 1 هفته- 2 هفته و همانطور مرور

کلمات قبلی باید ادامه داشته باشد. و فاصله این دوره ها مدام بیشتر و بیشتر می شود همانند یک فنر که درابتدا به هم فشرده است و بازتر می شود.

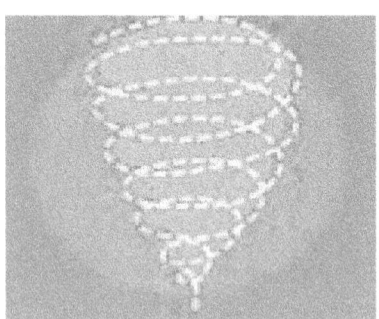

ب) مدل پیمسلر (Pimsleur)

همانند مدل آکسفورد، مدل دیگری برای دوره کردن مطالب وجود دارد. تحقیقات پیمسلر(1976) نشان می دهد که فاصله بین دوره ها باید بیشتر شود. دوره کردن مطالب یا لغات جدید براساس این مدل براساس به توان رساندن است و این بدان معنا است که اگر برای اولین بار 5 ثانیه بعد از خواندن یک کلمه آن را بخواهید مرور کنید، زمان مرور بعدی باید 5^2 باشد که می شود 25 ثانیه، زمان مرور بعدی 125=5^3 یعنی 125 ثانیه است والی آخر که در جدول زیر برای شما زمان 11 مرتبه تکرار آورده شده است.

Repetition	1	2	3	4	5	6	7	8	9	10	11
Time spacing before the next repetition	5 secs	25 secs	2 mins	10 mins	1 hour	5 hours	1 day	5 days	25 days	4 months	2 years

یادداشت برداری

یکی از نکات مهم در یادگیری، یادداشت برداری صحیح است. یادداشت برداری می تواند از یک کتاب و یا از سخنان استاد در هنگام تدریس در کلاس باشد.
یادداشت برداری امری کاملاً شخصی است ممکن است از یک مطلب ذکر شده هر دانشجویی نکات مختلفی یادداشت کند، اگر شما نمی توانید به خوبی نکات گفته شده سر کلاس را یادداشت کنید با در نظر گرفتن نکات زیر می توانید پیشرفت زیادی داشته باشید. قبل از آن به سوالات زیر پاسخ دهید. جواب سوالات زیر نشان می دهد شما چگونه یادداشت برداری می کنید.

1. چه موقع یادداشت برداری می کنید؟ سرکلاس، یا هنگام مطالعه؟
2. آیا یادداشت برداری برای شما سخت است یا آسان؟ اگر سخت است چرا؟
3. آیا هرگز از دوستانتان جزوه گرفته اید؟
4. آیا برای یادداشت برداری جملات را کامل می نویسید؟
5. آیا فکر می کنید یادداشت برداری در نمرات شما اثر دارد؟

حال به نکات زیر برای یادداشت بردای توجه کنید :
اولاً: به سخنان استاد خوب گوش دهید به برنامه دیروز یا فردا فکر نکنید.
دوماً : از نکات مهم سخنان استاد یادداشت بردارید.
سوماً: برای خود سیستمی برای یادداشت بردای داشته باشید .
چهارماً : باید یادداشت ها را فوراً مرور کنید، که در فصل های بعد در مورد مرور کردن توضیح داده خواهد شد .
در قسمت مهارت خواندن متون انگلیسی به خلاصه نویسی و پیدا کردن جملات اصلی پرداخته خواهد شد.
برای یادداشت برداری از کتاب می توانید از حاشیه های کتاب هم استفاده کنید و یادداشت ها را آنجا بنویسید. علاوه بر آن هنگام مطالعه کتاب می توان زیر نکات کلیدی و مهم آن خط کشید .
برای یادداشت برداری باید از شکل کوتاه کلمات استفاده کرد می توانید برای خود کلمات مخفف بسازید.

تکنیکهای تمرکز

چگونه بیشتر تمرکز کنیم؟

برای اینکه هنگام مطالعه تمرکز بیشتری داشته باشید و مطالب را بهتر متوجه شوید در یک مکان ثابت درس بخوانید. از لحاظ روان شناسی اگر در یک مکان ثابت درس بخوانید مغز شما شرطی شده و الگویی می سازد که به طور خودکار ذهن شما فعال تر شده و یادگیری بهتر خواهد بود.

شاید شما فکر کنید که بهتر است هنگام مطالعه به موسیقی ملایمی گوش دهید، اما تجربه ثابت کرده است اگر شما در یک مکان آرام درس بخوانید نتیجه بهتری خواهید گرفت.

زیرا درک مطلب رابطه مستقیمی با صداهای اطراف دارد به عبارت دیگر هر چه سر و صدای اطراف بیشتر باشد درک مطلب پایین تر است.

هرگز در تخت خواب مطالعه نکنید، زیرا حس خوابیدن در تخت خواب و مطالعه، با هم در تضاد است .

تمام کتابها و لوازم مورد نیاز را در نزدیکی خود قرار داده تا هیچ چیزی باعث به هم خوردن تمرکز شما نشود .

کتاب را با زاویه 30 درجه به سمت خود نگه دارید این موقعیت از حالتی که کتاب را روی سطح صاف قرار می دهید، بهتر است. در مکانی بنشینید که نور و هوای کافی داشته باشد.

ممکن است در مراحل اولیه تمرکز کردن مشکل باشد اما با انجام تمرینات ذکر شده به مرور آسان می شود و با کسب نمرات بهتر نتیجه آن مشخص می گردد.

تکنیکهایی برای حافظه بهتر و فراموشی کمتر

حافظه

شاید بارها تجربه کرده اید که قبل از امتحان ساعت های متوالی درس خوانده اید اما در نهایت نمره خوبی نداشته و از بیدار ماندن در شب قبل از امتحان تنها خستگی، اضطراب و پراکندگی افکار نصیبتان شده است .

موفق نشدن در امتحان به این دلیل است که اگر شما تمام مطالب را بخواهید شب قبل از امتحان بیاموزید فقط می توانید ٪20 از مطالب را در امتحان به خاطر بیاورید. برای اینکه بتوانید در امتحان موفق باشید باید ابتدا از کارکرد حافظه آگاه شوید .

به یادآوری مطالب و کاربرد مغز را می توان به 4 لایه تقسیم کرد:

-لایه اول درحافظه کوتاه مدت است. مثلاً وقتی شما معنی کلمه ای را برای اولین بار یاد می گیرید و آن را چند مرتبه تکرار می کنید. اما اگر فردا از شما خواسته شود که معنی آن کلمه را دوباره بیان کنید ممکن است نتوانید- این نشان دهنده آن است که معنی کلمه در حافظه کوتاه مدت باقی مانده و از بین رفته است.

-لایه دوم برای به یاد سپاری مطالب برای مدت طولانی تراست. مثلاً اگر اعلام شود که تاریخ امتحان زبان 4 روز بعد است و استاد آن تاریخ را چند مرتبه تکرار کند تاریخ امتحان به لایه دوم وارد می شود. این حالت بیشتر به مطالعه دروس در شب امتحان شباهت دارد. به عبارت دیگر مطالبی که در شب امتحان خوانده می شود به لایه دوم رفته و به احتمال زیاد قدرت به یادآوردن آن را نخواهید داشت.

-لایه سوم که به تکرار مطالب ونوشتن آن بستگی دارد، روش مناسبی برای یادگیری مطالب است. زیرا با نوشتن مطالب ماهیچه های شما به شما کمک می کند که مطالب را بهتر در ذهن نگه دارید وچشم شما نیز تصویری از مطالب گرفته و باعث می شود بخاطر آوری آنها راحت تر باشد.

-لایه چهارم که بهترین لایه است برای نگهداری مطالب است با تکرار و یادداشت برداری توام می شود. شما باید یادداشتها را مطابق الگوی تکرار که در قسمتهای بعد توضیح داده شده است، تکرار کنید.

پس بهتر است فقط در شب قبل از امتحان به بررسی و خواندن مطالب نپردازید وحداقل 2 یا 3 روز قبل از امتحان مطالب مورد نظر را دوره کنید.

نمودار فراموشی ابینگهایس (Ebbinghaus)

دوره کردن سیستماتیک و اساسی از عوامل مهم یادگیری لغات و مطالب جدید است. زیرا ابینگهایس (1884) نشان داده که 20 دقیقه پس از یادگیری یک مطلب، تقریباً 80٪ از آن فراموش می شود.

همانطور که در نمودار زیر نشان داده شده است. بیشترین میزان فراموشی تا 20 دقیقه پس از یادگیری مطالب (برای اولین بار) است، فراموشی تا 8 ساعت و 24 ساعت بعد باز هم اتفاق می افتد اما پس از 24 ساعت میزان فراموشی یکسان باقی می ماند، یعنی مطالب دیگر در ذهن باقی مانده و میزان فراموشی ثابت می ماند.

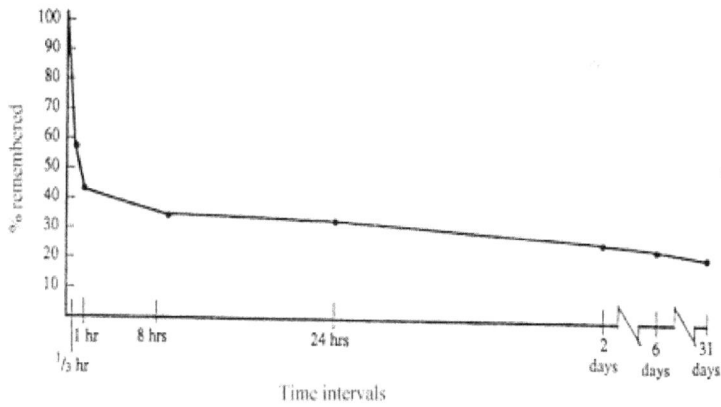

بنابراین برای اینکه مطالب بهتر آموخته شود و فراموش نشود 2 کار باید انجام داد. اول

انتخاب بهترین تکنیک برای مطالعه و سپس دوره کردن اصولی .
از همین رو با توجه به مطالب ارائه شده خواندن تمام مطالب در شب قبل از امتحان تنها وقت شما را هدر می دهد. زیرا حافظه شما نمی تواند تمام مطالب را نگه دارد. بهتر است مطالب جمع آوری شده در طی سال را یک هفته قبل از امتحان دوره کنید.

تکنیکهای امتحان

امتحان

برای اینکه در امتحان نمره بهتری بگیرید، بهتر است از نحوه و چگونگی امتحان مطلع شوید سپس مطالب و نوشته های سرکلاس را جمع کرده و آنها را به مرور دوره کنید. شب امتحان باید خوب بخوابید و خواب کافی داشته باشید و روز امتحان را با خوردن صبحانه ای مقوی آغاز نمایید.

اضطراب امتحان

بسیاری از دانشجویان بدلیل اضطراب امتحان ممکن است نتوانند به خوبی به سوالات پاسخ داده و نمره آنها کمتر از نمره واقعی شان شود.
پرسشنامه زیر یک نمونه پرسشنامه اضطراب امتحان است. با جواب دادن به این سوالات می توانید دریابید که آیا ترس و یا اضطراب امتحان در شما وجود دارد یا خیر .

مقیاس اضطراب امتحان ساراسون

این تست به شما کمک می کند که خود را بهتر بشناسید. از آنجایی که هیچ دو نفری شبیه به هم نیستند، پاسخ صحیح به سوالات، پاسخی است که از نظر شما صحیح است. شما به 37 سوال [عبارت] پاسخ خواهید داد. در مقابل هر سوال دو مربع کوچک در نظر گرفته شده است. با گذاشتن علامت ضربدر در یکی از مربع ها پاسخی که وضع شما را بهتر نشان می دهد، مشخص کنید. در پاسخ به سوالات به نکات زیر توجه کنید.

زمان پاسخگویی به سوالات محدود نیست، اما به سرعت پاسخ دهید و اولین پاسخی که به نظرتان می رسد، انتخاب کنید و برای هر سوال وقت زیادی صرف نکنید هیچ کدام از سوالات را از قلم نیندازید و برای هریک از سوالات یکی از دو پاسخ را انتخاب کنید. پاسخ واقعی و صادقانه به سوالات به شما کمک می کند خود را بهتر بشناسید. مشخصات خود را در محل تعیین شده بنویسید و پاسخ به سوالات را شروع کنید.

نام ونام خانوادگی : ....   سن :

جنسیت : مرد/زن

سوالات	درست	غلط
1) وقتی در یک امتحان مهم حاضر می شوم، به این فکر می کنم که شاگردان دیگر چقدر از من زرنگ ترند .		
2) اگر قرار باشد تست هوش بدهم قبل از تست نگران خواهم بود .		
3) اگر قرار باشد دریک آزمون هوش شرکت کنم، اعتماد واحساس آرامش خواهم داشت .		
4) شرکت در یک امتحان مهم ، برایم سخت است .		
5) وقتی که یک درس را امتحان می دهم ، به چیزهایی فکر می کنم که به آن درس ارتباط ندارد .		
6) وقتی استادی می خواهد بدون اطلاع قبلی امتحان بگیرد، نگران می شوم .		
7) وقتی به سوالات امتحانی پاسخ می دهم ، به نتایج شکست در امتحان فکر می کنم		
8) بعد از امتحانات مهم ، معمولا آنقدر عصبی هستم که دچار حالت تهوع می شوم.		
9) وقتی فکر می کنم قرار است در امتحان هوش یا امتحانات نهایی شرکت کنم، بدنم یخ می کند.		
10) گرفتن نمره خوب در یکی از امتحانات اعتماد به نفس مرا در امتحانات دیگر افزایش نمی دهد .		
11) درجریان امتحانات مهم ، گاهی احساس می کنم قلبم به شدت می زند.		
12) بعد از امتحان دادن معمولا حس می کنم که بهتر می توانستم جواب سوالات را بدهم .		
13) معمولا بعد از یک امتحان افسرده می شوم .		
14) قبل از امتحانات نهایی، احساس ناآرامی وآشفتگی می کنم.		
15) موقع امتحان، حالت های هیجانی من، درنتیجه امتحان اثر نمی گذارد.		
16) وقتی امتحان می دهم، آنقدر عصبی می شوم که چیزهایی را که واقعا بلد هستم ، فراموش می کنم.		
17) فکر می کنم که علت شکست من درامتحانات خودم هستم.		
18) هر چه بیشتر برای امتحان بخوانم بیشتر گیج می شوم .		
19) به محض اینکه یک امتحان تمام می شود ، سعی می کنم که دیگر درباره آن نگران نباشم ، اما موفق نمی شوم.		
20) گاهی درموقع امتحانات، از خودم می پرسم، آیا در امتحانات قبول می شوم؟		
21) ترجیح می دادم برای قبول شدن دریک درس ، یک مقاله بنویسم، به جای این که در امتحان شرکت کنم .		
22) ای کاش امتحانات اینقدر مرا اذیت نمی کرد .		

	23) فکر می کنم که نتایج امتحانات من بهتر می شد اگر که می توانستم به تنهایی امتحان دهم و محدودیت زمانی نداشتم.
	24) فکر کردن درباره نمره امتحان، بر درس خواندن ونتیجه امتحان من اثر می گذارد.
	25) فکر می کنم اگر امتحان نبود، بیشتر یاد می گرفتم .
	26) وقتی سرجلسه امتحان می روم، به خود می گویم : اگر حالا چیزی بلد نباشم، نباید نگران شوم .
	27) واقعا نمی فهمم که چرا بعضی از مردم از امتحان دادن ناراحت می شوند.
	28) فکر این که نتوانم خوب امتحان بدهم ، درنتیجه امتحانم اثر می گذارد .
	29) برای امتحانات پایان ترم کمتر از امتحانات میان ترم درس می خوانم.
	30) حتی اگر برای امتحان کاملا آماده باشم، باز هم شدیدا احساس اضطراب می کنم.
	31) قبل از شرکت در یک امتحان مهم ، از خوردن غذا لذت نمی برم.
	32) قبل از یک امتحان مهم دستانم می لرزد .
	33) کمتر اتفاق می افتد که قبل از امتحان، نیاز به آماده شدن برای آن امتحان را احساس کنم.
	34) مسئولین دانشگاه باید بدانند بعضی از دانشجویان بیشتر از برخی دیگر اضطراب دارند و همین امر می تواند در نمره امتحانات آنان تاثیر بگذارد.
	35) به نظرم امتحانات نباید باعث ناراحتی و تنش باشند .
	36) وقتی نتایج امتحانات را می خواهم بگیرم احساس بدی دارم .
	37) جرات ندارم که درسی بگیرم که استادان آن عادت دارند امتحانات کلاسی بگیرند.

نمره دهی به این پرسشنامه آسان است. پس از پر کردن پرسشنامه تعداد جواب هایی که در ستون درست علامت زده اید را جمع کنید. اگر نمره شما کمتر از 12 بود شما اضطراب امتحان ندارید یا اضطراب امتحان شما کم است. اگر نمره شما بین 20-12 بود اضطراب امتحان شما در حد متوسط است و نمره بالاتر از 20 نشان می دهد، شما اضطراب امتحان بالایی رنج می برید.

راههای موثری برای کاهش اضطراب در این کتاب معرفی شده است، اما اگر با انجام این دستورات بهتر نشدید باید به یک روانپزشک مراجعه کنید.

برای مقابله با اضطراب امتحان دستور العمل های زیر را به کار برید .

1. به اندازه کافی بخوابید.
2. قبل از امتحان غذای مناسب بخورید و از خوردن غذاهای چرب و نوشیدنی هایی مانند قهوه بپرهیزید .
3. ورزش کنید .
4. دوش بگیرید .

5. به موقع از خانه خارج شوید تا به موقع به جلسه امتحان برسید و نگران دیر شدن نباشید .
6. قبل از امتحان با دوستانتان مطالب را دوره کنید. البته این یک قانون کلی نیست زیرا بعضی از دانشجویان بیشتر مطالب را فراموش می کنند و این باعث آشفتگی ذهن آنان می شود.
7. اگر دوست دارید کتاب را ورق زده و نکات مهم را بخوانید و اگر این کار باعث ایجاد اضطراب در شما می شود آن را انجام ندهید.
8. مثبت فکر کنید و با خود تکرار کنید: شما هم مانند دیگران در این آزمون موفق می شوید.

هنگام جواب دادن به سوالات نکات زیر را در نظر داشته باشید:

1. ابتدا به سوالاتی جواب دهید که پاسخ آنرا می دانید، این به شما اعتماد به نفس می دهد.
2. اگر دیگران مشغول جواب دادن سوالات هستند به آنها توجه نکنید و خود را به خاطر فراموش کردن سوالات سرزنش نکنید .
3. اگر دوستان شما زودتر به تمام سوالات جواب دادند نگران نشوید و شما هم سعی کنید که وقت خود را تنظیم کنید .
4. به سوالات تستی قبل از سوالات تشریحی جواب دهید .
5. اگر سوالات نمره منفی ندارند، بصورت شانسی جواب دهید، زیرا در سوالات درست و غلط شانس جواب درست ۵۰٪ و در سوالات تستی ۲۵٪ می باشد.
6. تنها جواب سوالات را زمانی عوض کنید که مطمئن هستید جواب آنها اشتباه است .
7. در سوالات تستی اگر جواب سوال را نمی دانید جواب هایی را که اشتباه هستند حذف کنید. سپس بین بقیه گزینه ها یکی را انتخاب کنید.

تکنیکهای استفاده از دیکشنری

دیکشنری به ما چه می آموزد؟

یکی از مشکلات اساسی دانشجویان این است که طرز صحیح استفاده از دیکشنری را نمی دانند، آنها غالباً برای یافتن معنی کلمات مستقیماً به سراغ دیکشنری های انگلیسی به فارسی می روند، دیکشنری های انگلیسی به فارسی هرچند هم که خوب و مناسب باشند اما نمی توانند تمامی اطلاعاتی را که در دیکشنری انگلیسی به انگلیسی وجود دارد انتقال دهند.

استفاده صحیح از دیکشنری به شما کمک می کند که هم گنجینه لغات شما افزایش یافته هم از لحاظ تلفظ و گرامر پیشرفت کنید .

تمام دیکشنری ها با هم مشابه نیستند و تفاوت های جزیی دارند اما موارد زیر در تمام دیکشنری ها یکسان است .

- تمام دیکشنری ها به ترتیب حروف الفبای انگلیسی یعنی از A تا Z می باشد .
حال حروف به هم ریخته زیر را به ترتیب حروف الفبای مرتب کنید.

B f g a q s w t m p k x y h I r

- سیلاب (Syllabication)
- صرف (Inflected form)

- گرامر کلمات مانند (Part of speech) :

n. noun   v. verb   adj. adjective   pron. Pronoun   conj. Conjunction

- تلفظ کلمات (pronunciation)
- فشار (Stress)
- معنی کلمه (meaning)
- اصطلاحات (Idiom)
- تفاوت ها (Variants)

حال کلمات زیر را در جای مناسب در دیکشنری بنویسید.

Main entry	inflected forms	part of speech
Pronunciation	syllabication	guide word

مهارتها - چگونه با یادگیری تکنیکها، دانشجو و زبان آموز بهتری باشیم

analyst

right track and I think in the final analysis people will understand that... Violence in the last analysis produces more violence.

analyst /ˈænəlɪst/ (**analysts**) [1] An **analyst** is a person whose job is to analyse a subject and give opinions about it. ❑ ...a political analyst. [2] An **analyst** is someone, usually a doctor, who examines and treats people who are emotionally disturbed.

analytic /ˌænəˈlɪtɪk/ **Analytic** means the same as **analytical**. [mainly AM]

analytical /ˌænəˈlɪtɪkəl/ [1] An **analytical** way of doing something involves the use of logical reasoning. ❑ I have an analytical approach to every survey. ♦ **analytically** /ˌænəˈlɪtɪkli/ A teacher can encourage children to think analytically. [2] **Analytical** research involves using chemical analysis. ❑ All raw materials are subjected to our latest analytical techniques.

analyze /ˈænəlaɪz/ → see **analyse**.

anarchic /æˈnɑːkɪk/ If you describe someone or something as **anarchic**, you disapprove of them because they do not recognize or obey any rules or laws. ❑ ...anarchic attitudes and complete disrespect for authority.

anarchism /ˈænəkɪzəm/ **Anarchism** is the belief that the laws and power of governments should be replaced by people working together freely.

anarchist /ˈænəkɪst/ (**anarchists**) [1] An **anarchist** is a person who believes in anarchism. ❑ ...a well-known anarchist poet. [2] If someone has **anarchist** beliefs or views, they believe in anarchism. ❑ He was apparently quite converted from his anarchist views. [3] If you say that someone is an **anarchist**, you disapprove of them because they seem to pay no attention to the rules or laws that everyone else obeys. ❑ He was a social anarchist.

anarchistic /ˌænəˈkɪstɪk/ [1] An **anarchistic** person believes in anarchism. **Anarchistic** activity or literature promotes anarchism. ❑ ...an anarchistic revolutionary movement. [2] If you describe someone as **anarchistic**, you disapprove of them because they pay no attention to the rules or laws that everyone else obeys. ❑ The Hell's Angels were once the most notorious and anarchistic of motorbike gangs.

anarcho- /ˈænəkoʊ-/ **Anarcho-** combines with nouns and adjectives to form words indicating that something is both anarchistic and the other thing that is mentioned. ❑ In France there was a long tradition of anarcho-syndicalism.

anarchy /ˈænəki/ If you describe a situation as **anarchy**, you mean that nobody seems to be paying any attention to rules or laws. ❑ Civil war and famine sent the nation plunging into anarchy.

anathema /əˈnæθəmə/ If something is **anathema to** you, you strongly dislike it. ❑ Violence was anathema to him.

anatomical /ˌænəˈtɒmɪkəl/ **Anatomical** means relating to the structure of the bodies of people and animals. ❑ ...minute anatomical differences between insects. ♦ **anatomically** /ˌænəˈtɒmɪkli/ I need my pictures to be anatomically correct.

anatomist /əˈnætəmɪst/ (**anatomists**) An **anatomist** is an expert in anatomy.

anatomize /əˈnætəmaɪz/ (**anatomizes, anatomizing, anatomized**)
☑ in BRIT, also use **anatomise**

If you **anatomize** a subject or an issue, you examine it in great detail. [FORMAL] ❑ The magazine is devoted to anatomizing the inadequacies of liberalism.

anatomy /əˈnætəmi/ (**anatomies**) [1] **Anatomy** is the study of the structure of the bodies of people or animals. [2] You can refer to your body as your **anatomy**. [HUMOROUS] [3] An animal's **anatomy** is the structure of its body.

ancillary

ancestor /ˈænsestə/ (**ancestors**) [1] Your **ancestors** are the people from whom you are descended. ❑ ...our daily lives, so different from those of our ancestors... He could trace his ancestors back seven hundred years. [2] An **ancestor** of something modern is an earlier thing from which it developed. ❑ The direct ancestor of the modern cat was the Kaffir cat of ancient Egypt.

ancestral /ænˈsestrəl/ You use **ancestral** to refer to a person's family in former times, especially when the family is important and has property or land which they have had for a long time. ❑ ...the family's ancestral home in southern Germany.

ancestry /ˈænsestri/ (**ancestries**) Your **ancestry** is the fact that you are descended from certain people. ❑ ...a family who could trace their ancestry back to the sixteenth century.

anchor /ˈæŋkə/ (**anchors, anchoring, anchored**) [1] An **anchor** is a heavy hooked object that is dropped from a boat into the water at the end of a chain in order to make the boat stay in one place. [2] When a boat **anchors** or when you **anchor** it, its anchor is dropped into the water in order to make it stay in one place. ❑ We could anchor off the pier... They anchored the boat. [3] If you **anchor** an object somewhere, you fix it to something to prevent it moving from that place. ❑ The roots anchor the plant in the earth... The child seat belt was not properly anchored to the car. [4] If you **anchor** a television or radio programme, especially a news programme, you are the person who presents it and acts as a link between interviews and reports which come from other places or studios. [mainly AM] ❑ Viewers saw him anchoring a five-minute summary of regional news. ...a series of cassettes on the Vietnam War, anchored by Mr. Cronkite. [5] The **anchor** on a television or radio programme, especially a news programme, is the person who presents it. [mainly AM] ❑ He worked in the news division of ABC — he was the anchor of its 15-minute evening newscast. [6] If a boat is **at anchor**, it is floating in a particular place and is prevented from moving by its anchor.

anchorage /ˈæŋkərɪdʒ/ (**anchorages**) An **anchorage** is a place where a boat can anchor safely. ❑ The nearest safe anchorage was in Halifax, Nova Scotia... The vessel yesterday reached anchorage off Dubai.

anchorman /ˈæŋkəmæn/ (**anchormen**) also **anchor man**. The **anchorman** on a television or radio programme, especially a news programme, is the person who presents it.

anchorwoman /ˈæŋkəwʊmən/ (**anchorwomen**) The **anchorwoman** on a television or radio programme, especially a news programme, is the woman who presents it.

anchovy /ˈæntʃəvi, AM -tʃoʊvi/ (**anchovies**) Anchovies are small fish that live in the sea. They are often eaten salted.

ancien regime /ɑ̃sjɛ̃ reɪʒiːm/ [1] The **ancien regime** was the political and social system in France before the revolution of 1789. [2] If a country has had the same political system for a long time and you disapprove of it, you can refer to it as **the ancien regime**.

ancient /ˈeɪnʃənt/ [1] **Ancient** means belonging to the distant past, especially to the period in history before the end of the Roman Empire. ❑ They believed ancient Greece and Rome were vital sources of learning. ♦ **anciently** Salisbury Plain was known anciently as Ellendune. [2] **Ancient** means very old, or having existed for a long time. ❑ ...ancient Jewish tradition.

ancient history Ancient history is the history of ancient civilizations, especially Greece and Rome.

ancillary /ænˈsɪləri, AM ˈænsəleri/ (**ancillaries**) [1] The **ancillary** workers in an institution are the people such as cleaners and cooks whose work supports the main work of the institution. ❑ ...an

19

لازم به ذکر است که برای یادگیری تلفظ صحیح کلمات باید IPA (International Phonetic alphabet) یا الفبای آوانگار بین الملل آموخته شود.

با مراجعه به جداول زیر تلفظ کلمات مختلف را تمرین کنید.

vowels	
IPA	**Examples**
ʌ	cup, luck
ɑ:	arm, father
æ	cat, black
e	met, bed
ə	away, cinema
ɜ:ʳ	turn, learn
ɪ	hit, sitting
i:	see, heat
ɒ	hot, rock
ɔ:	call, four
ʊ	put, could
u:	blue, food
Diphtongue	
aɪ	five, eye
aʊ	now, out
eɪ	say, eight
oʊ	go, home
ɔɪ	boy, join
eəʳ	where, air
ɪəʳ	near, here
ʊəʳ	pure, tourist

مهارتها - چگونه با یادگیری تکنیکها، دانشجو و زبان آموز بهتری باشیم

	consonants
IPA	**Examples**
b	*b*ad, la*b*
d	*d*id, la*d*y
f	*f*ind, i*f*
g	*g*ive, fla*g*
h	*h*ow, *h*ello
j	*y*es, *y*ellow
k	*c*at, ba*ck*
l	*l*eg, *litt*le
m	*m*an, le*m*on
n	*n*o, te*n*
ŋ	si*ng*, fi*n*ger
p	*p*et, ma*p*
r	*r*ed, t*r*y
s	*s*un, mi*ss*
ʃ	*sh*e, cra*sh*
t	*t*ea, ge*tt*ing
tʃ	*ch*eck, *ch*urch
θ	*th*ink, bo*th*
ð	*th*is, mo*th*er
v	*v*oice, fi*v*e
w	*w*et, *w*indow
z	*z*oo, la*z*y
ʒ	plea*s*ure, vi*s*ion
dʒ	*j*ust, lar*g*e

تکنیک یادگیری لغات

لغات

برای اینکه بین دو نفر ارتباط برقرار شود ساده ترین راه از طریق واژگان است . اگر کسی گرامر زبان انگلیسی را بلد نباشد می تواند با کلمات مفهوم سخن خود را منتقل کند. بنابراین یادگیری واژگان از اهمیت ویژه ای برخوردار است.

حتماً بارها با این مشکل مواجه شده اید که هنگام مطالعه انگلیسی واژگان را فراموش کرده اید و در نتیجه نتوانسته اید جمله را کامل و پیام خود را برسانید فکر می کنید چند واژه انگلیسی می دانید؟ البته جواب این سوال کمی پیچیده و مبهم است که خارج از بحث این کتاب می باشد.

چگونه می توانیم حجم لغات را افزایش دهیم؟ این سوالی است که بارها و بارها شنیده می شود. برای اینکه به دامنه لغات خود بیافزایید نکات زیر را در نظر بگیرید.

1. تا آنجا که می توانید مطالعه کنید .
2. می توانید از کتاب های داستان ساده تر شروع کنید و ابتدا معنی کلمات را از متن حدس بزنید سپس معنی آنها را با دیکشنری چک کند .
3. از دیکشنری استفاده کنید .
4. حتماً کلمات را در دیکشنری پیدا کنید و به معنی آن، تلفظ ، نکات گرامری و مثالی که برای آن آورده شده دقت کنید.
5. برنامه های رادیویی و تلویزیونی زبان اصلی گوش کنید .
6. پس از آنکه کلمات جدید را پیدا کردید و با معنی آن آشنا شدید باید با استفاده از راه کارهایی آن را به حافظه طولانی مدت بسپارید. چرا که دانستن معنی کلمه ای با به کار بردن آن کلمه در زمان مناسب متفاوت است، شما حتماً بارها تجربه کرده اید که

وقتی متنی را می خوانید ممکن است معنی کلمه ای به ذهن شما آشنا بیاید اما در هنگام صحبت کردن نتوانید آن کلمه و واژه را به کار ببرید.

برای دوره کردن لغات استفاده از جدول روش مناسبی است. جداول زیر نمونه دوره کردن لغاتی است که به تازگی آموخته اید.

ابتدا برای خودتان صفحه هایی مانند جداول زیر تهیه کنید.

ماهانه	هفتگی	روزانه	5 ساعت
		Zeal	Zeal
		Provoke	Provoke
		Helmet	Helmet
		Prophecy	Prophecy
		Negotiate	Negotiate

فرض کنید 5 کلمه ای که در جدول نوشته شده، کلمات جدید است. 5 ساعت بعد از یادگیری کلمات آنها را دوباره مرور کنید. اگر تمام کلمات را یاد گرفته بودید آنها را به ستون بعدی یعنی ستون روزانه ببرید. تا روز بعد دوباره آنها را مرور کنید. اما اگر بعضی از آنها را یاد نگرفته اید آنها را در همان ستونی 5 ساعت نگه دارید.

ماهانه	هفتگی	روزانه	5 ساعت
	zeal		
			provoke
	helmet		
			prophecy
	negotiate		

روز بعد دوباره تمام کلمات را دوره کنید. کلماتی که را یاد گرفته اید به ستون بعدی یعنی هفته ای انتقال دهید اما آنهایی را که فراموش کرده اید به ستون قبلی یعنی 5 ساعت انتقال دهید.

ماهانه	هفتگی	روزانه	5 ساعت
zeal			
			provoke
		helmet	
			prophecy
negotiate			

تا آخر همین کار را ادامه دهید وکلماتی را که یاد گرفته اید به ستون بعد منتقل کنید و آنهایی را که فراموش کرده اید به ستون قبل تا مجدداً وارد مرحله مرور کردن شوند. این کار را تا زمانی که تمام کلمات را یاد بگیرید تکرار کنید.

استراتژی های زیر نیز برگرفته از مدل پیشنهادی خانم ربکا آکسفورد(1990)، بهترین راه برای به خاطر سپاری واژگان می باشد.

1-کلمات را دسته بندی کنید و کلماتی که معنای مرتبط با یک موضوع را دارند در یک جا قرار دهید. مانند:

- Weather   (hot - cold – rainy – stormy – windy - snowy)
- parts of body (hand – foot – nose – chest – leg - neck)
- vehicles   (car – bus – cab – train – truck - lorry)

2-تصویری از کلمات در ذهن خود بسازید.

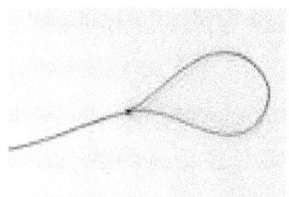

loop　　　　　　　summit

3-کلمات را به پیشوند و پسوندهایش بشکنید. با یادگیری پیشوند و پسوند ها حجم لغات شما افزایش می یابد بی آنکه بخواهید معنی همه کلمات را بدانید. مانند:

- Microscope: (micro-=small; -scope=look)
- Telescope: (tele-=far; -scope=look)
- Locomotive: (loco-=place; -mot-=move; -ive= adjective maker, 'full of')
- Geography: (geo-=earth; -graphy=writing)

4-زیر کلمات جدید خط بکشید یا آنها را بصورت رنگی نشان دهید.

The next day, Mr. Willie Walker, the new teacher, appeared in our class. He was very **slender**, with close-cropped hair and neatly dressed. He looked at all the students one by one then distributed a number of papers among the students. Right at that moment the front window **shattered** and everybody rushed into the school yard without paying attention to the teacher. Mr. Walker was shocked, he was the last one who **grasped** the rest of the papers and ran into the yard.

5-معنی کلمات جدید را براساس موضوع حدس بزنید. گاهی دیکشنری دراختیار شما نیست پس باید سعی کنید براساس موضوع بحث و کنش زبانی خودتان معنی کلمات جدید را حدس بزنید. مانند:

Example: You must spend less until your *debts* are paid off.
Example: The test was not easy. In fact, to me, it was so *complicated*.

برای یادگیری لغات علاوه براستراتژی های گفته شده می توان از روش های زیر هم استفاده کرد.

1) کلمات را با شعر و آواز یاد بگیرید. Parrot with my Carrot.

2- مکانی را در ذهن خود مجسم کنید مانند یک اتاق و سپس نام وسایلی که در آن است بخاطر بسپارید.

3- هر کلمه جدید را به یک انگشت دست ربط داده و یاد بگیرید.

4- با کلمات جدید داستان جالب وخنده داری بسازید. به این صورت کلمات را بهتر یاد می گیرید.

پر بسامد ترین کلمات

تعداد لغاتی که هر شخص می داند نشان دهنده سطح تحصیلات و معلومات او است. انگلیسی زبانان به طور متوسط در هر سال 1000 لغت به گنجینه لغات خود می افزایند که این اندازه با حجم لغات افراد غیر انگلیسی زبان متفاوت است.

حال که روش های یادگیری لغات را آموخته اید باید بدانید چه لغاتی را بیاموزید. اگر به دیکشنری وبستر (Webster) که کامل ترین دیکشنری است مراجعه نمایید می بینید که 54000 لغت در آن وجود دارد. از بین این همه لغت یادگیری کدام یک بهتر است؟ در سال 1990 نیشن (Nation) کلمات را براساس بسامد آنها تقسیم بندی کرد. به عقیده او 1000 کلمه پر بسامد اول ٪72 از هر متنی را شامل می شود. با یادگیری پر بسامدترین کلمات می توانید درک مطلب بالایی داشته باشید. لیست این کلمات به همراه کلمات دانشگاهی (کلماتی که برای خواندن کتاب دانشگاهی به زبان انگلیسی لازم است) در ضمیمه آمده است.

جدول زیر نشان دهنده تعداد لغات و پوشش متنی آن می باشد.

تعداد لغات	پوشش متنی (درصد)
1000	72
2000	79/7
3000	84
4000	86/8
5000	88/7
6000	89/9
15851	97/8

تکنیکهای خواندن

خواندن

در مورد مهارت خواندن مهم این است که در ابتدا مشخص شود، هدف شما از خواندن چیست؟

گاهی شما برای رفع خستگی و تفریح مطالعه می کنید و گاهی برای امتحان، بنابراین هدف از مطالعه متفاوت است و در نتیجه سرعت مطالعه نیز متفاوت می باشد.

سرعت مطالعه می تواند شامل سرعت های زیر باشد :

1- بسیار سریع / 400 کلمه در دقیقه برای خواندن کتابهای غیر درسی، داستانی و رمانها.

2- سریع / 350 در دقیقه برای مطالعه جزوه های نسبتاً آسان.

3- متوسط / 250 کلمه در دقیقه برای خواندن جزوه های آسان.

4- کند / 200 کلمه در دقیقه برای اینکه جزئیات مطلب نیز خوانده شود.

برای اینکه سرعت خواندن را محاسبه کنید باید از فرمول زیر استفاده نمایید.

```
1- تعداد خطوط

2- تعداد کلمات در هر خط  X
   _____
3- کل کلمات خوانده شده

4- کل کلمات خوانده شده
```

```
5- تعداد دقیقه ÷
————————————
6- میزان خواندن در دقیقه
```

به عنوان مثال شما یک متن 100 خطی را در 3 دقیقه خوانده اید که در هر خط 6 کلمه وجود داشته است. اگر این اعداد را در فرمول بالا بگذارید و زمان شروع و پایان خواندن متن نیز یادداشت شده باشد می توانید سرعت مطالعه را بدست آورید.

```
100 تعداد خطوط
6 تعداد کلمات در هر خط x
————————————
600 کل کلمات خوانده شده


600 کل کلمات خوانده شده
3 تعداد دقیقه ÷
————————————
200 میزان خواندن در دقیقه
```

یعنی میزان خواندن شما 200 کلمه در دقیقه است که بسته به هدف مطالعه تفسیر آن متغیر است.

(Scanning) اجمالی خواندن، (skimming) با دقت خواندن

یکی از تکنیکهایی که در هنگام مطالعه متن به کار می رود skimming , Scanning کردن است.

در روش scanning شما باید به سرعت از مطالب بگذرید تا به نکته یا مطالب مورد نظر خود برسید، مثلاً یک بخش از کتاب را به سرعت مرور می کنید تا سال تولد شخصی را پیدا کنید.

در روش skimming شما به سرعت متن یا پاراگراف را می خوانید تا فهم کلی از آن بدست آورید. حالا متن زیر را خوانده و با روش skim, scan کردن سوالات را جواب دهید.

What's On?

First read the following questions and then use the TV Schedule to find the answers.

1. Jack has a video - can he watch both documentaries without having to make a video?
2. Is there a show about making good investments?
3. You are thinking about traveling to the USA for a vacation. Which show should you watch?
4. Your friend doesn't have a TV, but would like to watch a film starring Tom Cruise. Which film should you record on your video?
5. Peter is interested in wild animals which show should he watch?
6. Which sport can you watch that takes place outside?
7. Which sport can you watch that takes place inside?
8. You like modern art. Which documentary should you watch?
9. How often can you watch the news?
10. Is there a horror film on this evening?

TV Schedule

CBC	FNB	ABN
6.00 p.m.: **National News** - join Jack Parsons for your daily news roundup. 6.30: **The Tiddles**- Peter joins Mary for a wild adventure in the park. 7.00: **Golf Review**- Watch highlights from today's final round of the Grand Master's.	6.00 p.m.: **In-Depth News** - In-depth coverage of the most important national and international news stories. 7.00: **Nature Revealed**- Interesting documentary taking a look at the microscopic universe in your average speck of dust. 7.30: **Ping - Pong Masters**- Live coverage from Peking. 9.30: **It's**	6.00 p.m.: **Travel Abroad** - This week we travel to sunny California! 6.30: **The Flintstones**- Fred and Barney are at it again. 7.00: **Pretty Boy**- Tom Cruise, the prettiest boy of them all, in an action packed thriller about Internet espionage.

8.30: **Shock from the Past**- This entertaining film by Arthur Schmidt takes a poke at the wild side of gambling.
10.30: **Nightly News**- A review of the day's most important events.
11.00: **MOMA: Art for Everyone**- A fascinating documentary that helps you enjoy the difference between pointilism and video installations.
12:00: **Hard Day's Night**- Reflections after a long, hard day.

Your Money- That's right and this favorite game show could make or break you depending on how you place your bets.
10.30: **Green Park**- Stephen King's latest monster madness. 0.30: **Late Night News**- Get the news you need to get a hard start on the upcoming day.

9.00: **Tracking the Beast**- The little understood wildebeest filmed in its natural surroundings with commentary by Dick Signit.
10.00: **Pump Those Weights**- A guide to successfully using weights to develop your physique while getting fit.
11.30: **The Three Idiots**- A fun farce based on those three tenors who don't know when to call it quits.
1.00: **National Anthem**- Close the day with this salute to our country.

اما خواندن بدون درک مطلب ارزشی ندارد. حال برای بالا بردن سرعت خواندن و درک مطلب بیشتر، متن زیر را بخوانید.

Reading skills for academic study: Skimming for gist

Exercise 1

Read the first sentence of each paragraph in the following text.

THE PERSONAL QUALITIES OF A TEACHER

Here I want to try to give you an answer to the question: What personal qualities are desirable in a teacher? Probably no two people would draw up exactly similar lists, but I think the following would be generally accepted.

First, the teacher's personality should be pleasantly live and attractive. This does not rule out people who are physically plain, or even ugly, because many such have great personal charm. But it does rule out such types as the over-excitable, melancholy, frigid, sarcastic, cynical, frustrated, and over-bearing : I would say too, that it excludes all of dull or purely negative personality. I still stick to what I said in my earlier book: that school children probably 'suffer more from bores than from brutes'.

Secondly, it is not merely desirable but essential for a teacher to have a genuine capacity for sympathy - in the literal meaning of that word; a capacity to tune in to the minds and feelings of other people, especially, since most teachers are school teachers, to the minds and feelings of children. Closely related with this is the capacity to be tolerant - not, indeed, of what is wrong, but of the frailty and immaturity of human nature which induce people, and again especially children, to make mistakes.

Thirdly, I hold it essential for a teacher to be both intellectually and morally honest. This does not mean being a plaster saint. It means that he will be aware of his intellectual strengths, and limitations, and will have thought about and decided upon the moral principles by which his life shall be guided. There is no contradiction in my going on to say that a teacher should be a bit of an actor. That is part of the technique of teaching, which demands that every now and then a teacher should be able to put on an act - to enliven a lesson, correct a fault, or award praise. Children, especially young children, live in a world that is rather larger than life.

A teacher must remain mentally alert. He will not get into the profession if of low intelligence, but it is all too easy, even for people of above-average intelligence, to stagnate intellectually - and that means to deteriorate intellectually. A teacher must be quick to adapt himself to any situation, however improbable and able to improvise, if necessary at less than a moment's notice. (Here I should stress that I use 'he' and 'his' throughout the book simply as a matter of convention and convenience.)

On the other hand, a teacher must be capable of infinite patience. This, I may say, is largely a matter of self-discipline and self-training; we are none of us born like that. He must be pretty resilient; teaching makes great demands on nervous energy. And he should be able to take in his stride the innumerable petty irritations any adult dealing with children has to endure.

Finally, I think a teacher should have the kind of mind which always wants to go on learning. Teaching is a job at which one will never be perfect; there is always something more to learn about it. There are three principal objects of study: the subject, or subjects, which the teacher is teaching; the methods by which they can best be taught to the particular pupils in the classes he is teaching; and - by far the most important - the children, young people, or adults to whom they are to be taught. The two cardinal principles of British education today are that education is education of the whole person, and that it is best acquired through full and active co-operation between two persons, the teacher and the learner.

(From *Teaching as a Career,* by H. C. Dent, Batsford, 1961)

Notice how reading these sentences gives you a good idea about the meaning of the text: six qualities of a teacher. If you need more details, read the text again.

در بار اول مدت زمان مطالعه و نمره کسب شده از درک مطلب متون مختلف را یادداشت نمایید. هر روز این کار را انجام دهید تا سرعت و دقت مطالعه بالا رود. می توانید نتایج بدست آمده را در جدول زیر وارد نمایید.

	1	2	3	4	5	6	7	8	9	10
زمان										
نمره										

سپس نمرات به دست آمده را با جدول زیر بررسی کنید.

نتیجه خواندن و درک مطلب

صفحه نمایش	کاغذ	درک مطلب	نتیجه خواندن	
100 wpm	110 wpm	50%	Insufficient	نا کافی
200 wpm	240 wpm	60%	Average reader	متوسط
300 wpm	400 wpm	80%	Good reader	خوب
700 wpm	1000 wpm	85%	Excellent reader	عالی

توجه داشته باشید که سرعت مطالعه از صفحه کامپیوتر 25٪ کند تر از صفحه کتاب است.

تکنیکهای نوشتن

نوشتن

مهارت نوشتن یک متن با مهارت یادداشت برداری از کتاب ومهارت خواندن مرتبط است. به عبارت دیگر پایه و اصل تمام این مهارتها طرح (outlining) است. اگر هنگام مطالعه یا برای خلاصه نویسی یا حتی برای نوشتن مطالب جدید آنها را دسته بندی کرده و به صورت منظم ارائه دهید، هم مطالب بهتر در ذهن شما می ماند و هم نوشته های منسجم تری ارائه می شود.

درآزمونهای تافل وایلتس از شما خواسته می شود که برای یک عنوان و یا مطلب ارائه شده، متن کامل بنویسید. بنابراین شما ابتدا باید طرح کار را در نظر بگیرید. برای مهارت خواندن هم همینطور است. زیرا خواندن و نوشتن مانند دو روی یک سکه است. اگر نویسنده ای از طرح استفاده کند و نوشته خود را ارائه دهد، خواننده نیز می تواند با استفاده از همان طرح به مفهوم مطلب نوشته شده دست یابد.

شکل ظاهری طرح به صورت زیر است.

I.****************************
 A.***************************
 B.***************************
II.****************************
 A.***************************

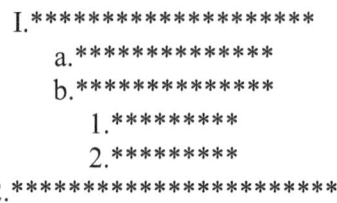

برای مثال در نظر بگیرید که از شما خواسته شده است در مورد ترافیک بنویسید. شما به نکات زیر اشاره می کنید.

Traffic is problem because
    Too many cars
    Narrow streets
    Dreivers don't obey regulations

وسپس ایده های خود را بسط می دهید.

Traffic has recently become a serious problem in the capital of my country. There are three reasons first, the number of automobiles has doubled in the past five years, with the result that there are more cars than the streets can accommodate. Second, the streets are old and narrow. Because there are few garages or parking lots, there narrow streets are made narrower by the cars that parked alongside. Third, many drivers do not obey the regulations, so that many traffic jams result from cars going the wrong way on a one-way street.

یکی دیگر از تکنیکهایی که در نوشتن و در خواندن مورد استفاده قرار می گیرد پیدا کردن مطلب اصلی (main idea) است. معمولاً جمله اول هر پاراگراف شامل جمله اصلی می شود وجملات بعدی حمایت کننده (supporting idea) هستند. به نمودار زیر دقت کنید.

Main idea xxxxxxxxxxxxxxxxxxxxxxxxxxxxxxxxxxxxxxxxxxx

Supporting idea xxxxxxxxxxxxxxxxxxxxxxxxxxxxxxxxxxxxx

Supporting idea xxxxxxxxxxxxxxxxxxxxxxxxxxxxxxxxxxxxx

همانطور که در نمودار بالا مشخص است جمله اول مطلب اصلی وجملات بعدی حمایت کننده هستند.

تکنیکهای صحبت کردن و گوش دادن

صحبت کردن و گوش دادن

برای اینکه مهارت صحبت کردن در زبان انگلیسی را شروع کنید، باید بسیار بخوانید و بسیار گوش دهید. دراین حالت شما مانند کودکی هستید که می خواهد زبان مادری خود را بیاموزد پس ابتدا با گوش دادن به اطرافیان صداها و کلمات را بیاموزید.

از جملات ساده شروع کنید و آن را بسط دهید. اگر در آزمون های تافل یا ایلتس ساختاری را بلد نبودید از ساختار دیگری بجای آن استفاده نمایید واگر جمله ای را اشتباه گفتید آن را تصحیح کنید. اگر کلمه یا ساختاری را فراموش کردید می توانید از کلماتی مانند now, okay و um و یا oh استفاده کنید.

در مورد مهارت گوش دادن نیز همینطور- باید بسیار گوش دهید و هنگام گوش دادن دقت کنید و مطالب را خلاصه کنید.

درابتدا ممکن است شما هیچ متوجه نشوید. پس از نوشتن کلمات و یا صداهایی که متوجه می شوید آغاز کنید.

باید تمرین زیادی داشته باشید. خواندن کتابهای گرامری مانند English grammar in USE که دارای سه سطح مختلف مقدماتی (beginner) و متوسط (intermediate) و پیشرفته (advanced) می باشد می تواند کمک موثری در یادگیری گرامر زبان انگلیسی باشد. هرگز نکات گرامری زبان انگلیسی را با فارسی مقایسه نکنید و آن را همانگونه که هست یاد بگیرید.

اگر می خواهید در یادگیری زبان موفق باشید باید هر روز ساعت معینی را برای آن صرف کنید و تمرین کنید.

منابع انگلیسی

Broukal, M. (2007). *TOFEL grammar flash*. Canada: Peterson's Thomson Learning.

Broukal, M. (2007). *TOFEL reading flash*. Canada: Peterson's Thomson Learning.

Broukal, M. (2007). *TOFEL word flash*. Canada: Peterson's Thomson Learning.

Broulkal, M., & Nolan- Woods, E. (2006).*NTC's prepration for the TOEFL*.U.S.A.: NTC Publishing Group.

Coman, M. J. (2008). *How to improve your study skills*. U.S.A. : NTC Publishing Group.

Common prefix, suffix and root words. Retrieved 2010 from, https://www.msu.edu/~defores1/gre/roots/gre_rts_afx2.htm.

English proficiency test. Retrieved 2010 from,

http://www.transparent.com/learn-english/proficiency-test.html

Sharpe, P. J. (2007) (12th edition). *TOEFL iBT test*. U.S.A: Barrons.

Yourkey, C. R. (2007). *Study skills*. U.S.A: McGraw Hill, Inc.

Nation, I.S.P. (1990). *Teaching and learning vocabulary*. New York: Newbury House.

Oxford, R. L. (1990). *Language learning strategies*: *What every teacher should know*. New York: Newbury House.

Pimsleur. P. (1976). A memory schedule. *Modern Language Journal*, **51**, 73-75.

Sarason, I.G. (1980). Test anxiety: Theory, research, and applications. Permission granted by Lawrence Erlbaum Associates, Inc.

Instant Words

1,000 Most Frequently Used Words

These are the most common words in English, ranked in frequency order. The first 25 make up about a third of all printed material. The first 100 make up about half of all written material, and the first 300 make up about 65 percent of all written material. Is it any wonder that all students must learn to recognize these words instantly and to spell them correctly also?

Source: The Reading Teacher's Book of Lists, Fourth Edition, © 2000 by Prentice Hall

Authors: Fry, Kress & Fountoukidis

The 1000 Most Common Words in English
FIRST HUNDRED

Words 1-25	Words 26-50	Words 51-75	Words 76-100
the	or	will	number
of	one	up	no
and	had	other	way
a	by	about	could
to	word	out	people
in	but	many	my
is	not	then	than
you	what	them	first
that	all	these	water
it	were	so	been
he	we	some	call
was	when	her	who
for	your	would	oil
on	can	make	its
are	said	like	now
as	there	him	find
with	use	into	long
his	an	time	down
they	each	has	day
I	which	look	did
at	she	two	get
be	do	more	come
this	how	write	made
have	their	go	may
from	if	see	part

The 1000 Most Common Words in English
SECOND HUNDRED

Words 101-125	Words 126-150	Words 151-175	Words 176-200
over	say	set	try
new	great	put	kind
sound	where	end	hand
take	help	does	picture
only	through	another	again
little	much	well	change
work	before	large	off
know	line	must	play
place	right	big	spell
year	too	even	air
live	mean	such	away
me	old	because	animal
back	any	turn	house
give	same	here	point
most	tell	why	page
very	boy	ask	letter
after	follow	went	mother
thing	came	men	answer
our	want	read	found
just	show	need	study
name	also	land	still
good	around	different	learn
sentence	form	home	should
man	three	us	America
think	small	move	world

The 1000 Most Common Words in English
THIRD HUNDRED

Words 201-225	Words 226-250	Words 251-275	Words 276-300
high	saw	important	miss
every	left	until	idea
near	don't	children	enough
add	few	side	eat
food	while	feet	face
between	along	car	watch
own	might	mile	far
below	close	night	Indian
country	something	walk	really
plant	seem	white	almost
last	next	sea	let
school	hard	began	above
father	open	grow	girl
keep	example	took	sometimes
tree	begin	river	mountain
never	life	four	cut
start	always	carry	young
city	those	state	talk
earth	both	once	soon
eye	paper	book	list
light	together	hear	song
thought	got	stop	being
head	group	without	leave
under	often	second	family
story	run	later	it's

The 1000 Most Common Words in English
FOURTH HUNDRED

Words 301-325	Words 326-350	Words 351-375	Words 376-400
body	order	listen	farm
music	red	wind	pulled
color	door	rock	draw
stand	sure	space	voice
sun	become	covered	seen
question	top	fast	cold
fish	ship	several	cried
area	across	hold	plan
mark	today	himself	notice
dog	during	toward	south
horse	short	five	sing
birds	better	step	war
problem	best	morning	ground
complete	however	passed	fall
room	low	vowel	king
knew	hours	true	town
since	black	hundred	I'll
ever	products	against	unit
piece	happened	pattern	figure
told	whole	numeral	certain
usually	measure	table	field
didn't	remember	north	travel
friends	early	slowly	wood
easy	waves	money	fire
heard	reached	map	upon

The 1000 Most Common Words in English
FIFTH HUNDRED

Words 401-425	Words 426-450	Words 451-475	Words 476-500
done	decided	plane	filled
English	contain	system	heat
road	course	behind	full
halt	surface	ran	hot
ten	produce	round	check
fly	building	boat	object
gave	ocean	game	am
box	class	force	rule
finally	note	brought	among
wait	nothing	understand	noun
correct	rest	warm	power
oh	carefully	common	cannot
quickly	scientists	bring	able
person	inside	explain	six
became	wheels	dry	size
shown	stay	though	dark
minutes	green	language	ball
strong	known	shape	material
verb	island	deep	special
stars	week	thousands	heavy
front	less	yes	fine
feel	machine	clear	pair
fact	base	equation	circle
inches	ago	yet	include
street	stood	government	built

The 1000 Most Common Words in English

SIXTH HUNDRED

Words 501-525	Words 526-550	Words 551-575	Words 576-600
can't	picked	legs	beside
matter	simple	sat	gone
square	cells	main	sky
syllables	paint	winter	glass
perhaps	mind	wide	million
bill	love	written	west
felt	cause	length	lay
suddenly	rain	reason	weather
test	exercise	kept	root
direction	eggs	interest	instruments
center	train	arms	meet
farmers	blue	brother	third
ready	wish	race	months
anything	drop	present	paragraph
divided	developed	beautiful	raised
general	window	store	represent
energy	difference	job	soft
subject	distance	edge	whether
Europe	heart	past	clothes
moon	sit	sign	flowers
region	sum	record	shall
return	summer	finished	teacher
believe	wall	discovered	held
dance	forest	wild	describe
members	probably	happy	drive

The 1000 Most Common Words in English
SEVENTH HUNDRED

Words 601-625	Words 626-650	Words 651-675	Words 676-700
cross	already	hair	rolled
speak	instead	age	bear
solve	phrase	amount	wonder
appear	soil	scale	smiled
metal	bed	pounds	angle
son	copy	although	fraction
either	free	per	Africa
ice	hope	broken	killed
sleep	spring	moment	melody
village	case	tiny	bottom
factors	laughed	possible	trip
result	nation	gold	hole
jumped	quite	milk	poor
snow	type	quiet	let's
ride	themselves	natural	fight
care	temperature	lot	surprise
floor	bright	stone	French
hill	lead	act	died
pushed	everyone	build	beat
baby	method	middle	exactly
buy	section	speed	remain
century	lake	count	dress
outside	consonant	cat	iron
everything	within	someone	couldn't
tall	dictionary	sail	fingers

The 1000 Most Common Words in English
EIGHTH HUNDRED

Words 701-725	Words 726-750	Words 751-775	Words 776-800
row	president	yourself	caught
least	brown	control	fell
catch	trouble	practice	team
climbed	cool	report	God
wrote	cloud	straight	captain
shouted	lost	rise	direct
continued	sent	statement	ring
itself	symbols	stick	serve
else	wear	party	child
plains	bad	seeds	desert
gas	save	suppose	increase
England	experiment	woman	history
burning	engine	coast	cost
design	alone	bank	maybe
joined	drawing	period	business
foot	east	wire	separate
law	pay	choose	break
ears	single	clean	uncle
grass	touch	visit	hunting
you're	information	bit	flow
grew	express	whose	lady
skin	mouth	received	students
valley	yard	garden	human
cents	equal	please	art
key	decimal	strange	feeling

The 1000 Most Common Words in English
NINTH HUNDRED

Words 801-825	Words 826-850	Words 851-875	Words 876-900
supply	guess	thick	major
corner	silent	blood	observe
electric	trade	lie	tube
insects	rather	spot	necessary
crops	compare	bell	weight
tone	crowd	fun	meat
hit	poem	loud	lifted
sand	enjoy	consider	process
doctor	elements	suggested	army
provide	indicate	thin	hat
thus	except	position	property
won't	expect	entered	particular
cook	flat	fruit	swim
bones	seven	tied	terms
tail	interesting	rich	current
board	sense	dollars	park
modern	string	send	sell
compound	blow	sight	shoulder
mine	famous	chief	industry
wasn't	value	Japanese	wash
fit	wings	stream	block
addition	movement	planets	spread
belong	pole	rhythm	cattle
safe	exciting	eight	wife
soldiers	branches	science	sharp

The 1000 Most Common Words in English

TENTH HUNDRED

Words 901-925	Words 926-950	Words 951-975	Words 976-1000
company	sister	gun	total
radio	oxygen	similar	deal
we'll	plural	death	determine
action	various	score	evening
capital	agreed	forward	nor
factories	opposite	stretched	rope
settled	wrong	experience	cotton
yellow	chart	rose	apple
isn't	prepared	allow	details
southern	pretty	fear	entire
truck	solution	workers	corn
fair	fresh	Washington	substances
printed	shop	Greek	smell
wouldn't	suffix	women	tools
ahead	especially	bought	conditions
chance	shoes	led	cows
born	actually	march	track
level	nose	northern	arrived
triangle	afraid	create	located
molecules	dead	British	sir
France	sugar	difficult	seat
repeated	adjective	match	division
column	fig	win	effect
western	office	doesn't	underline
church	huge	steel	view

2,000 Most Frequently Used Words

The 2000 Most Common Words in English

n = noun | v = verb | adj = adjective | adv = adverb | det = determiner | prep = preposition

Words 1-40	Words 41-80	Words 81-120
a (det)	advice (n)	amongst (prep)
ability (n)	advise (v)	amount (n)
able (adj)	affair (n)	an (det)
about (adv)	affect (v)	analysis (n)
about (prep)	afford (v)	ancient (adj)
above (adv)	afraid (adj)	and conj
above (prep)	after conj	animal (n)
absence (n)	after (prep)	announce (v)
absolutely (adv)	afternoon (n)	annual (adj)
academic (adj)	afterwards (adv)	another (det)
accept (v)	again (adv)	answer (n)
access (n)	against (prep)	answer (v)
accident (n)	age (n)	any (det)
accompany (v)	agency (n)	anybody pron
according to (prep)	agent (n)	anyone pron
account (n)	ago (adv)	anything pron
account (v)	agree (v)	anyway (adv)
achieve (v)	agreement (n)	apart (adv)
achievement (n)	ahead (adv)	apparent (adj)
acid (n)	aid (n)	apparently (adv)
acquire (v)	aim (n)	appeal (n)
across (prep)	aim (v)	appeal (v)
act (n)	air (n)	appear (v)
act (v)	aircraft (n)	appearance (n)
action (n)	all (adv)	application (n)
active (adj)	all (det)	apply (v)
activity (n)	allow (v)	appoint (v)
actual (adj)	almost (adv)	appointment (n)
actually (adv)	alone (adj)	approach (n)
add (v)	alone (adv)	approach (v)
addition (n)	along (adv)	appropriate (adj)
additional (adj)	along (prep)	approve (v)
address (n)	already (adv)	area (n)
address (v)	alright (adv)	argue (v)
administration (n)	also (adv)	argument (n)
admit (v)	alternative (adj)	arise (v)
adopt (v)	alternative (n)	arm (n)
adult (n)	although conj	army (n)
advance (n)	always (adv)	around (adv)
advantage (n)	among (prep)	around (prep)

The 2000 Most Common Words in English

n = noun | v = verb | adj = adjective | adv = adverb | det = determiner | prep = preposition

Words 121-160	Words 161-200	Words 201-240
arrange (v)	away (adv)	beside (prep)
arrangement (n)	aye (interjection)	best (adv)
arrive (v)	baby (n)	better (adv)
art (n)	back (adv)	between (prep)
article (n)	back (n)	beyond (prep)
artist (n)	background (n)	big (adj)
as (adv)	bad (adj)	bill (n)
as conj	bag (n)	bind (v)
as (prep)	balance (n)	bird (n)
ask (v)	ball (n)	birth (n)
aspect (n)	band (n)	bit (n)
assembly (n)	bank (n)	black (adj)
assess (v)	bar (n)	block (n)
assessment (n)	base (n)	blood (n)
asset (n)	base (v)	bloody (adj)
associate (v)	basic (adj)	blow (v)
association (n)	basis (n)	blue (adj)
assume (v)	battle (n)	board (n)
assumption (n)	be (v)	boat (n)
at (prep)	bear (v)	body (n)
atmosphere (n)	beat (v)	bone (n)
attach (v)	beautiful (adj)	book (n)
attack (n)	because conj	border (n)
attack (v)	become (v)	both (adv)
attempt (n)	bed (n)	both (det)
attempt (v)	bedroom (n)	bottle (n)
attend (v)	before (adv)	bottom (n)
attention (n)	before conj	box (n)
attitude (n)	before (prep)	boy (n)
attract (v)	begin (v)	brain (n)
attractive (adj)	beginning (n)	branch (n)
audience (n)	behaviour (n)	break (v)
author (n)	behind (prep)	breath (n)
authority (n)	belief (n)	bridge (n)
available (adj)	believe (v)	brief (adj)
average (adj)	belong (v)	bright (adj)
avoid (v)	below (adv)	bring (v)
award (n)	below (prep)	broad (adj)
award (v)	beneath (prep)	brother (n)
aware (adj)	benefit (n)	budget (n)

The 2000 Most Common Words in English

n = noun | v = verb | adj = adjective | adv = adverb | det = determiner | prep = preposition

Words 241-280	Words 281-320	Words 321-360
build (v)	chair (n)	coal (n)
building (n)	chairman (n)	code (n)
burn (v)	challenge (n)	coffee (n)
bus (n)	chance (n)	cold (adj)
business (n)	change (n)	colleague (n)
busy (adj)	change (v)	collect (v)
but conj	channel (n)	collection (n)
buy (v)	chapter (n)	college (n)
by (prep)	character (n)	colour (n)
cabinet (n)	characteristic (n)	combination (n)
call (n)	charge (n)	combine (v)
call (v)	charge (v)	come (v)
campaign (n)	cheap (adj)	comment (n)
can modal	check (v)	comment (v)
candidate (n)	chemical (n)	commercial (adj)
capable (adj)	chief (adj)	commission (n)
capacity (n)	child (n)	commit (v)
capital (n)	choice (n)	commitment (n)
car (n)	choose (v)	committee (n)
card (n)	church (n)	common (adj)
care (n)	circle (n)	communication (n)
care (v)	circumstance (n)	community (n)
career (n)	citizen (n)	company (n)
careful (adj)	city (n)	compare (v)
carefully (adv)	civil (adj)	comparison (n)
carry (v)	claim (n)	competition (n)
case (n)	claim (v)	complete (adj)
cash (n)	class (n)	complete (v)
cat (n)	clean (adj)	completely (adv)
catch (v)	clear (adj)	complex (adj)
category (n)	clear (v)	component (n)
cause (n)	clearly (adv)	computer (n)
cause (v)	client (n)	concentrate (v)
cell (n)	climb (v)	concentration (n)
central (adj)	close (adj)	concept (n)
centre (n)	close (adv)	concern (n)
century (n)	close (v)	concern (v)
certain (adj)	closely (adv)	concerned (adj)
certainly (adv)	clothes (n)	conclude (v)
chain (n)	club (n)	conclusion (n)

The 2000 Most Common Words in English

n = noun | v = verb | adj = adjective | adv = adverb | det = determiner | prep = preposition

Words 361-400	Words 401-440	Words 441-480
condition (n)	council (n)	dead (adj)
conduct (v)	count (v)	deal (n)
conference (n)	country (n)	deal (v)
confidence (n)	county (n)	death (n)
confirm (v)	couple (n)	debate (n)
conflict (n)	course (n)	debt (n)
congress (n)	court (n)	decade (n)
connect (v)	cover (n)	decide (v)
connection (n)	cover (v)	decision (n)
consequence (n)	create (v)	declare (v)
conservative (adj)	creation (n)	deep (adj)
consider (v)	credit (n)	deep (adv)
considerable (adj)	crime (n)	defence (n)
consideration (n)	criminal (adj)	defendant (n)
consist (v)	crisis (n)	define (v)
constant (adj)	criterion (n)	definition (n)
construction (n)	critical (adj)	degree (n)
consumer (n)	criticism (n)	deliver (v)
contact (n)	cross (v)	demand (n)
contact (v)	crowd (n)	demand (v)
contain (v)	cry (v)	democratic (adj)
content (n)	cultural (adj)	demonstrate (v)
context (n)	culture (n)	deny (v)
continue (v)	cup (n)	department (n)
contract (n)	current (adj)	depend (v)
contrast (n)	currently (adv)	deputy (n)
contribute (v)	curriculum (n)	derive (v)
contribution (n)	customer (n)	describe (v)
control (n)	cut (n)	description (n)
control (v)	cut (v)	design (n)
convention (n)	damage (n)	design (v)
conversation (n)	damage (v)	desire (n)
copy (n)	danger (n)	desk (n)
corner (n)	dangerous (adj)	despite (prep)
corporate (adj)	dark (adj)	destroy (v)
correct (adj)	data (n)	detail (n)
cos conj	date (n)	detailed (adj)
cost (n)	date (v)	determine (v)
cost (v)	daughter (n)	develop (v)
could modal	day (n)	development (n)

The 2000 Most Common Words in English

n = noun | v = verb | adj = adjective | adv = adverb | det = determiner | prep = preposition

Words 481-520	Words 521-560	Words 561-600
device (n)	dress (v)	emerge (v)
die (v)	drink (n)	emphasis (n)
difference (n)	drink (v)	employ (v)
different (adj)	drive (n)	employee (n)
difficult (adj)	drive (v)	employer (n)
difficulty (n)	driver (n)	employment (n)
dinner (n)	drop (v)	empty (adj)
direct (adj)	drug (n)	enable (v)
direct (v)	dry (adj)	encourage (v)
direction (n)	due (adj)	end (n)
directly (adv)	during (prep)	end (v)
director (n)	duty (n)	enemy (n)
disappear (v)	each (det)	energy (n)
discipline (n)	ear (n)	engine (n)
discover (v)	early (adj)	engineering (n)
discuss (v)	early (adv)	enjoy (v)
discussion (n)	earn (v)	enough (adv)
disease (n)	earth (n)	enough (det)
display (n)	easily (adv)	ensure (v)
display (v)	east (n)	enter (v)
distance (n)	easy (adj)	enterprise (n)
distinction (n)	eat (v)	entire (adj)
distribution (n)	economic (adj)	entirely (adv)
district (n)	economy (n)	entitle (v)
divide (v)	edge (n)	entry (n)
division (n)	editor (n)	environment (n)
do (v)	education (n)	environmental (adj)
doctor (n)	educational (adj)	equal (adj)
document (n)	effect (n)	equally (adv)
dog (n)	effective (adj)	equipment (n)
domestic (adj)	effectively (adv)	error (n)
door (n)	effort (n)	escape (v)
double (adj)	egg (n)	especially (adv)
doubt (n)	either (adv)	essential (adj)
down (adv)	either (det)	establish (v)
down (prep)	elderly (adj)	establishment (n)
draw (v)	election (n)	estate (n)
drawing (n)	element (n)	estimate (v)
dream (n)	else (adv)	even (adv)
dress (n)	elsewhere (adv)	

The 2000 Most Common Words in English

n = noun | v = verb | adj = adjective | adv = adverb | det = determiner | prep = preposition

Words 601-640	Words 641-680	Words 681-720
event (n)	extremely (adv)	fill (v)
eventually (adv)	eye (n)	film (n)
ever (adv)	face (n)	final (adj)
every (det)	face (v)	finally (adv)
everybody pron	facility (n)	finance (n)
everyone pron	fact (n)	financial (adj)
everything pron	factor (n)	find (v)
evidence (n)	factory (n)	finding (n)
exactly (adv)	fail (v)	fine (adj)
examination (n)	failure (n)	finger (n)
examine (v)	fair (adj)	finish (v)
example (n)	fairly (adv)	fire (n)
excellent (adj)	faith (n)	firm (n)
except conj	fall (n)	first (adj)
exchange (n)	fall (v)	fish (n)
executive (n)	familiar (adj)	fit (v)
exercise (n)	family (n)	fix (v)
exercise (v)	famous (adj)	flat (n)
exhibition (n)	far (adj)	flight (n)
exist (v)	far (adv)	floor (n)
existence (n)	farm (n)	flow (n)
existing (adj)	farmer (n)	flower (n)
expect (v)	fashion (n)	fly (v)
expectation (n)	fast (adj)	focus (v)
expenditure (n)	fast (adv)	follow (v)
expense (n)	father (n)	following (adj)
expensive (adj)	favour (n)	food (n)
experience (n)	fear (n)	foot (n)
experience (v)	fear (v)	football (n)
experiment (n)	feature (n)	for conj
expert (n)	fee (n)	for (prep)
explain (v)	feel (v)	force (n)
explanation (n)	feeling (n)	force (v)
explore (v)	female (adj)	foreign (adj)
express (v)	few (det)	forest (n)
expression (n)	few (n)	forget (v)
extend (v)	field (n)	form (n)
extent (n)	fight (v)	form (v)
external (adj)	figure (n)	formal (adj)
extra (adj)	file (n)	former (det)

The 2000 Most Common Words in English

n = noun | v = verb | adj = adjective | adv = adverb | det = determiner | prep = preposition

Words 721-760	Words 761-800	Words 801-840
forward (adv)	good (adj)	help (n)
foundation (n)	good (n)	help (v)
free (adj)	government (n)	hence (adv)
freedom (n)	grant (n)	her (det)
frequently (adv)	grant (v)	her pron
fresh (adj)	great (adj)	here (adv)
friend (n)	green (adj)	herself pron
from (prep)	grey (adj)	hide (v)
front (adj)	ground (n)	high (adj)
front (n)	group (n)	high (adv)
fruit (n)	grow (v)	highly (adv)
fuel (n)	growing (adj)	hill (n)
full (adj)	growth (n)	him pron
fully (adv)	guest (n)	himself pron
function (n)	guide (n)	his (det)
fund (n)	gun (n)	his pron
funny (adj)	hair (n)	historical (adj)
further (adv)	half (det)	history (n)
future (adj)	half (n)	hit (v)
future (n)	hall (n)	hold (v)
gain (v)	hand (n)	hole (n)
game (n)	hand (v)	holiday (n)
garden (n)	handle (v)	home (adv)
gas (n)	hang (v)	home (n)
gate (n)	happen (v)	hope (n)
gather (v)	happy (adj)	hope (v)
general (adj)	hard (adj)	horse (n)
general (n)	hard (adv)	hospital (n)
generally (adv)	hardly (adv)	hot (adj)
generate (v)	hate (v)	hotel (n)
generation (n)	have (v)	hour (n)
gentleman (n)	he pron	house (n)
get (v)	head (n)	household (n)
girl (n)	head (v)	housing (n)
give (v)	health (n)	how (adv)
glass (n)	hear (v)	however (adv)
go (v)	heart (n)	huge (adj)
goal (n)	heat (n)	human (adj)
god (n)	heavy (adj)	human (n)
gold (n)	hell (n)	hurt (v)

The 2000 Most Common Words in English

n = noun | v = verb | adj = adjective | adv = adverb | det = determiner | prep = preposition

Words 841-880	Words 881-920	Words 921-960
husband (n)	influence (v)	itself pron
i pron	inform (v)	job (n)
idea (n)	information (n)	join (v)
identify (v)	initial (adj)	joint (adj)
if conj	initiative (n)	journey (n)
ignore (v)	injury (n)	judge (n)
illustrate (v)	inside (adv)	judge (v)
image (n)	inside (prep)	jump (v)
imagine (v)	insist (v)	just (adv)
immediate (adj)	instance (n)	justice (n)
immediately (adv)	instead (adv)	keep (v)
impact (n)	institute (n)	key (adj)
implication (n)	institution (n)	key (n)
imply (v)	instruction (n)	kid (n)
importance (n)	instrument (n)	kill (v)
important (adj)	insurance (n)	kind (n)
impose (v)	intend (v)	king (n)
impossible (adj)	intention (n)	kitchen (n)
impression (n)	interest (n)	knee (n)
improve (v)	interested (adj)	know (v)
improvement (n)	interesting (adj)	knowledge (n)
in (adv)	internal (adj)	labour (adj)
in (prep)	international (adj)	labour (n)
incident (n)	interpretation (n)	lack (n)
include (v)	interview (n)	lady (n)
including (prep)	into (prep)	land (n)
income (n)	introduce (v)	language (n)
increase (n)	introduction (n)	large (adj)
increase (v)	investigate (v)	largely (adv)
increased (adj)	investigation (n)	last (adj)
increasingly (adv)	investment (n)	last (v)
indeed (adv)	invite (v)	late (adj)
independent (adj)	involve (v)	late (adv)
index (n)	iron (n)	later (adv)
indicate (v)	island (n)	latter (det)
individual (adj)	issue (n)	laugh (v)
individual (n)	issue (v)	launch (v)
industrial (adj)	it pron	law (n)
industry (n)	item (n)	lawyer (n)
influence (n)	its (det)	lay (v)

59

The 2000 Most Common Words in English

n = noun | v = verb | adj = adjective | adv = adverb | det = determiner | prep = preposition

Words 961-1000	Words 1001-1040	Words 1041-1080
lead (n)	listen (v)	mark (n)
lead (v)	literature (n)	mark (v)
leader (n)	little (adj)	market (n)
leadership (n)	little (adv)	market (v)
leading (adj)	little (det)	marriage (n)
leaf (n)	live (v)	married (adj)
league (n)	living (adj)	marry (v)
lean (v)	loan (n)	mass (n)
learn (v)	local (adj)	master (n)
least (adv)	location (n)	match (n)
leave (v)	long (adj)	match (v)
left (adj)	long (adv)	material (n)
leg (n)	look (n)	matter (n)
legal (adj)	look (v)	matter (v)
legislation (n)	lord (n)	may modal
length (n)	lose (v)	may modal
less (adv)	loss (n)	maybe (adv)
less (det)	lot (n)	me pron
let (v)	love (n)	meal (n)
letter (n)	love (v)	mean (v)
level (n)	lovely (adj)	meaning (n)
liability (n)	low (adj)	means (n)
liberal (adj)	lunch (n)	meanwhile (adv)
library (n)	machine (n)	measure (n)
lie (v)	magazine (n)	measure (v)
life (n)	main (adj)	mechanism (n)
lift (v)	mainly (adv)	media (n)
light (adj)	maintain (v)	medical (adj)
light (n)	major (adj)	meet (v)
like (prep)	majority (n)	meeting (n)
like (v)	make (v)	member (n)
likely (adj)	male (adj)	membership (n)
limit (n)	male (n)	memory (n)
limit (v)	man (n)	mental (adj)
limited (adj)	manage (v)	mention (v)
line (n)	management (n)	merely (adv)
link (n)	manager (n)	message (n)
link (v)	manner (n)	metal (n)
lip (n)	many (det)	method (n)
list (n)	map (n)	middle (n)

The 2000 Most Common Words in English

n = noun | v = verb | adj = adjective | adv = adverb | det = determiner | prep = preposition

Words 1081-1120	Words 1121-1160	Words 1161-1200
might modal	name (v)	not (adv)
mile (n)	narrow (adj)	note (n)
military (adj)	nation (n)	note (v)
milk (n)	national (adj)	nothing pron
mind (n)	natural (adj)	notice (n)
mind (v)	nature (n)	notice (v)
mine (n)	near (prep)	notion (n)
minister (n)	nearly (adv)	now (adv)
ministry (n)	necessarily (adv)	nuclear (adj)
minute (n)	necessary (adj)	number (n)
miss (v)	neck (n)	nurse (n)
mistake (n)	need (n)	object (n)
model (n)	need (v)	objective (n)
modern (adj)	negotiation (n)	observation (n)
module (n)	neighbour (n)	observe (v)
moment (n)	neither (adv)	obtain (v)
money (n)	network (n)	obvious (adj)
month (n)	never (adv)	obviously (adv)
more (adv)	nevertheless (adv)	occasion (n)
more (det)	new (adj)	occur (v)
morning (n)	news (n)	odd (adj)
most (adv)	newspaper (n)	of (prep)
most (det)	next (adv)	off (adv)
mother (n)	next (det)	off (prep)
motion (n)	nice (adj)	offence (n)
motor (n)	night (n)	offer (n)
mountain (n)	no (adv)	offer (v)
mouth (n)	no (det)	office (n)
move (n)	no (interjection)	officer (n)
move (v)	no-one pron	official (adj)
movement (n)	nobody pron	official (n)
much (adv)	nod (v)	often (adv)
much (det)	noise (n)	oil (n)
murder (n)	none pron	okay (adv)
museum (n)	nor conj	old (adj)
music (n)	normal (adj)	on (adv)
must modal	normally (adv)	on (prep)
my (det)	north (n)	once (adv)
myself pron	northern (adj)	once conj
name (n)	nose (n)	one pron

The 2000 Most Common Words in English

n = noun | v = verb | adj = adjective | adv = adverb | det = determiner | prep = preposition

Words 1201-1240	Words 1241-1280	Words 1281-1320
only (adj)	pain (n)	phase (n)
only (adv)	paint (v)	phone (n)
onto (prep)	painting (n)	photograph (n)
open (adj)	pair (n)	physical (adj)
open (v)	panel (n)	pick (v)
operate (v)	paper (n)	picture (n)
operation (n)	parent (n)	piece (n)
opinion (n)	park (n)	place (n)
opportunity (n)	parliament (n)	place (v)
opposition (n)	part (n)	plan (n)
option (n)	particular (adj)	plan (v)
or conj	particularly (adv)	planning (n)
order (n)	partly (adv)	plant (n)
order (v)	partner (n)	plastic (n)
ordinary (adj)	party (n)	plate (n)
organisation (n)	pass (v)	play (n)
organise (v)	passage (n)	play (v)
organization (n)	past (adj)	player (n)
origin (n)	past (n)	please (adv)
original (adj)	past (prep)	pleasure (n)
other (adj)	path (n)	plenty pron
other (n)	patient (n)	plus (prep)
other pron	pattern (n)	pocket (n)
otherwise (adv)	pay (n)	point (n)
ought modal	pay (v)	point (v)
our (det)	payment (n)	police (n)
ourselves pron	peace (n)	policy (n)
out (adv)	pension (n)	political (adj)
outcome (n)	people (n)	politics (n)
output (n)	per (prep)	pool (n)
outside (adv)	percent (n)	poor (adj)
outside (prep)	perfect (adj)	popular (adj)
over (adv)	perform (v)	population (n)
over (prep)	performance (n)	position (n)
overall (adj)	perhaps (adv)	positive (adj)
own (det)	period (n)	possibility (n)
own (v)	permanent (adj)	possible (adj)
owner (n)	person (n)	possibly (adv)
package (n)	personal (adj)	post (n)
page (n)	persuade (v)	potential (adj)

The 2000 Most Common Words in English

n = noun | v = verb | adj = adjective | adv = adverb | det = determiner | prep = preposition

Words 1321-1360	Words 1361-1400	Words 1401-1440
potential (n)	project (n)	rapidly (adv)
pound (n)	promise (v)	rare (adj)
power (n)	promote (v)	rate (n)
powerful (adj)	proper (adj)	rather (adv)
practical (adj)	properly (adv)	reach (v)
practice (n)	property (n)	reaction (n)
prefer (v)	proportion (n)	read (v)
prepare (v)	propose (v)	reader (n)
presence (n)	proposal (n)	reading (n)
present (adj)	prospect (n)	ready (adj)
present (n)	protect (v)	real (adj)
present (v)	protection (n)	realise (v)
president (n)	prove (v)	reality (n)
press (n)	provide (v)	realize (v)
press (v)	provided conj	really (adv)
pressure (n)	provision (n)	reason (n)
pretty (adv)	pub (n)	reasonable (adj)
prevent (v)	public (adj)	recall (v)
previous (adj)	public (n)	receive (v)
previously (adv)	publication (n)	recent (adj)
price (n)	publish (v)	recently (adv)
primary (adj)	pull (v)	recognise (v)
prime (adj)	pupil (n)	recognition (n)
principle (n)	purpose (n)	recognize (v)
priority (n)	push (v)	recommend (v)
prison (n)	put (v)	record (n)
prisoner (n)	quality (n)	record (v)
private (adj)	quarter (n)	recover (v)
probably (adv)	question (n)	red (adj)
problem (n)	question (v)	reduce (v)
procedure (n)	quick (adj)	reduction (n)
process (n)	quickly (adv)	refer (v)
produce (v)	quiet (adj)	reference (n)
product (n)	quite (adv)	reflect (v)
production (n)	race (n)	reform (n)
professional (adj)	radio (n)	refuse (v)
profit (n)	railway (n)	regard (v)
program (n)	rain (n)	region (n)
programme (n)	raise (v)	regional (adj)
progress (n)	range (n)	regular (adj)

The 2000 Most Common Words in English

n = noun | v = verb | adj = adjective | adv = adverb | det = determiner | prep = preposition

Words 1441-1480	Words 1481-1520	Words 1521-1560
regulation (n)	result (v)	save (v)
reject (v)	retain (v)	say (v)
relate (v)	return (n)	scale (n)
relation (n)	return (v)	scene (n)
relationship (n)	reveal (v)	scheme (n)
relative (adj)	revenue (n)	school (n)
relatively (adv)	review (n)	science (n)
release (n)	revolution (n)	scientific (adj)
release (v)	rich (adj)	scientist (n)
relevant (adj)	ride (v)	score (v)
relief (n)	right (adj)	screen (n)
religion (n)	right (adv)	sea (n)
religious (adj)	right (n)	search (n)
rely (v)	ring (n)	search (v)
remain (v)	ring (v)	season (n)
remember (v)	rise (n)	seat (n)
remind (v)	rise (v)	second (n)
remove (v)	risk (n)	secondary (adj)
repeat (v)	river (n)	secretary (n)
replace (v)	road (n)	section (n)
reply (v)	rock (n)	sector (n)
report (n)	role (n)	secure (v)
report (v)	roll (v)	security (n)
represent (v)	roof (n)	see (v)
representation (n)	room (n)	seek (v)
representative (n)	round (adv)	seem (v)
request (n)	round (prep)	select (v)
require (v)	route (n)	selection (n)
requirement (n)	row (n)	sell (v)
research (n)	royal (adj)	send (v)
resource (n)	rule (n)	senior (adj)
respect (n)	run (n)	sense (n)
respond (v)	run (v)	sentence (n)
response (n)	rural (adj)	separate (adj)
responsibility (n)	safe (adj)	separate (v)
responsible (adj)	safety (n)	sequence (n)
rest (n)	sale (n)	series (n)
rest (v)	same (det)	serious (adj)
restaurant (n)	sample (n)	seriously (adv)
result (n)	satisfy (v)	servant (n)

The 2000 Most Common Words in English

n = noun | v = verb | adj = adjective | adv = adverb | det = determiner | prep = preposition

Words 1561-1600	Words 1601-1640	Words 1641-1680
serve (v)	simply (adv)	song (n)
service (n)	since conj	soon (adv)
session (n)	since (prep)	sorry (adj)
set (n)	sing (v)	sort (n)
set (v)	single (adj)	sound (n)
settle (v)	sir (n)	sound (v)
settlement (n)	sister (n)	source (n)
several (det)	sit (v)	south (n)
severe (adj)	site (n)	southern (adj)
sex (n)	situation (n)	space (n)
sexual (adj)	size (n)	speak (v)
shake (v)	skill (n)	speaker (n)
shall modal	skin (n)	special (adj)
shape (n)	sky (n)	species (n)
share (n)	sleep (v)	specific (adj)
share (v)	slightly (adv)	speech (n)
she pron	slip (v)	speed (n)
sheet (n)	slow (adj)	spend (v)
ship (n)	slowly (adv)	spirit (n)
shoe (n)	small (adj)	sport (n)
shoot (v)	smile (n)	spot (n)
shop (n)	smile (v)	spread (v)
short (adj)	so (adv)	spring (n)
shot (n)	so conj	staff (n)
should modal	social (adj)	stage (n)
shoulder (n)	society (n)	stand (v)
shout (v)	soft (adj)	standard (adj)
show (n)	software (n)	standard (n)
show (v)	soil (n)	star (n)
shut (v)	soldier (n)	star (v)
side (n)	solicitor (n)	start (n)
sight (n)	solution (n)	start (v)
sign (n)	some (det)	state (n)
sign (v)	somebody pron	state (v)
signal (n)	someone pron	statement (n)
significance (n)	something pron	station (n)
significant (adj)	sometimes (adv)	status (n)
silence (n)	somewhat (adv)	stay (v)
similar (adj)	somewhere (adv)	steal (v)
simple (adj)	son (n)	step (n)

The 2000 Most Common Words in English

n = noun | v = verb | adj = adjective | adv = adverb | det = determiner | prep = preposition

Words 1681-1720	Words 1721-1760	Words 1761-1800
step (v)	supply (v)	test (v)
stick (v)	support (n)	text (n)
still (adv)	support (v)	than conj
stock (n)	suppose (v)	thank (v)
stone (n)	sure (adj)	thanks (n)
stop (v)	surely (adv)	that conj
store (n)	surface (n)	that (det)
story (n)	surprise (n)	the (det)
straight (adv)	surround (v)	theatre (n)
strange (adj)	survey (n)	their (det)
strategy (n)	survive (v)	them pron
street (n)	switch (v)	theme (n)
strength (n)	system (n)	themselves pron
strike (n)	table (n)	then (adv)
strike (v)	take (v)	theory (n)
strong (adj)	talk (n)	there (adv)
strongly (adv)	talk (v)	there pron
structure (n)	tall (adj)	therefore (adv)
student (n)	tape (n)	these (det)
studio (n)	target (n)	they pron
study (n)	task (n)	thin (adj)
study (v)	tax (n)	thing (n)
stuff (n)	tea (n)	think (v)
style (n)	teach (v)	this (det)
subject (n)	teacher (n)	those (det)
substantial (adj)	teaching (n)	though (adv)
succeed (v)	team (n)	though conj
success (n)	tear (n)	thought (n)
successful (adj)	technical (adj)	threat (n)
such (det)	technique (n)	threaten (v)
suddenly (adv)	technology (n)	through (adv)
suffer (v)	telephone (n)	through (prep)
sufficient (adj)	television (n)	throughout (prep)
suggest (v)	tell (v)	throw (v)
suggestion (n)	temperature (n)	thus (adv)
suitable (adj)	tend (v)	ticket (n)
sum (n)	term (n)	time (n)
summer (n)	terms (n)	tiny (adj)
sun (n)	terrible (adj)	title (n)
supply (n)	test (n)	to (adv)

The 2000 Most Common Words in English

n = noun | v = verb | adj = adjective | adv = adverb | det = determiner | prep = preposition

Words 1801-1840	Words 1841-1880	Words 1881-1920
to infinitive-marker	trouble (n)	value (n)
to (prep)	true (adj)	variation (n)
today (adv)	trust (n)	variety (n)
together (adv)	truth (n)	various (adj)
tomorrow (adv)	try (v)	vary (v)
tone (n)	turn (n)	vast (adj)
tonight (adv)	turn (v)	vehicle (n)
too (adv)	twice (adv)	version (n)
tool (n)	type (n)	very (adj)
tooth (n)	typical (adj)	very (adv)
top (adj)	unable (adj)	via (prep)
top (n)	under (adv)	victim (n)
total (adj)	under (prep)	victory (n)
total (n)	understand (v)	video (n)
totally (adv)	understanding (n)	view (n)
touch (n)	undertake (v)	village (n)
touch (v)	unemployment (n)	violence (n)
tour (n)	unfortunately (adv)	vision (n)
towards (prep)	union (n)	visit (n)
town (n)	unit (n)	visit (v)
track (n)	united (adj)	visitor (n)
trade (n)	university (n)	vital (adj)
tradition (n)	unless conj	voice (n)
traditional (adj)	unlikely (adj)	volume (n)
traffic (n)	until conj	vote (n)
train (n)	until (prep)	vote (v)
train (v)	up (adv)	wage (n)
training (n)	up (prep)	wait (v)
transfer (n)	upon (prep)	walk (n)
transfer (v)	upper (adj)	walk (v)
transport (n)	urban (adj)	wall (n)
travel (v)	us pron	want (v)
treat (v)	use (n)	war (n)
treatment (n)	use (v)	warm (adj)
treaty (n)	used (adj)	warn (v)
tree (n)	used modal	wash (v)
trend (n)	useful (adj)	watch (v)
trial (n)	user (n)	water (n)
trip (n)	usual (adj)	wave (n)
	usually (adv)	way (n)

The 2000 Most Common Words in English

n = noun | v = verb | adj = adjective | adv = adverb | det = determiner | prep = preposition

Words 1921-1960	Words 1961-2000
we pron	wind (n)
weak (adj)	window (n)
weapon (n)	wine (n)
wear (v)	wing (n)
weather (n)	winner (n)
week (n)	winter (n)
weekend (n)	wish (v)
weight (n)	with (prep)
welcome (v)	withdraw (v)
welfare (n)	within (prep)
well (adv)	without (prep)
well (interjection)	woman (n)
west (n)	wonder (v)
western (adj)	wonderful (adj)
what (det)	wood (n)
whatever (det)	word (n)
when (adv)	work (n)
when conj	work (v)
where (adv)	worker (n)
where conj	working (adj)
whereas conj	works (n)
whether conj	world (n)
which (det)	worry (v)
while conj	worth (prep)
while (n)	would modal
whilst conj	write (v)
white (adj)	writer (n)
who pron	writing (n)
whole (adj)	wrong (adj)
whole (n)	yard (n)
whom pron	yeah (interjection)
whose (det)	year (n)
why (adv)	yes (interjection)
wide (adj)	yesterday (adv)
widely (adv)	yet (adv)
wife (n)	you pron
wild (adj)	young (adj)
will modal	your (det)
will (n)	yourself pron
win (v)	youth (n)

The Academic Word List (Averil Coxhead, 2000):
a list of 570 high-incidence and high-utility academic word families
for Secondary School, Higher Education, Career

There is a very important specialized vocabulary for learners intending to pursue academic studies in English at the secondary and post-secondary levels. The Academic Word List, compiled by Coxhead (2000), consists of 570 word families that are not in the most frequent 2,000 words of English but which occur reasonably frequently over a very wide range of academic texts. These 570 words are grouped into ten sublists that reflect word frequency and range. A word like analyze falls into Sublist 1, which contains the most frequent words, while the word adjacent falls into Sublist 10 which includes the least frequent (amongst this list of high incidence and high utility words). The following ten sublists contain the headwords of the families in the Academic Word List. In other words, the ten sublists contain the most frequent form of the word, more often a noun or verb form, although there may be one or more important related word forms. For example, the headword analyze would also include analyst, analytic, analytical and analytically in the word family.

The Academic Word List is not restricted to a specific field of study. That means that the words are useful for learners studying in disciplines as varied as literature, science, health, business, and law. This high utility academic word list does not contain technical words likely to appear in only one, specialized field of study such as amortization, petroglyph, onomatopoeia, or cartilage. Two-thirds of all academic English words come from Latin, French (through Latin), or Greek. Understandably, knowledge of the most high incidence and high utility academic words in English can significantly boost a student's comprehension level of school-based reading material. Secondary students who are taught these high-utility academic words and routinely placed in contexts requiring their usage are likely to be able to master academic material with more confidence and efficiency, wasting less time and energy in guessing words or consulting dictionaries than those who are only equipped with the most basic 2000-3000 words that characterize ordinary conversation.

Sources: Coxhead, Averil. (2000). A new academic word list. TESOL Quarterly, 34, 213-

The Academic Word List
Group 1

analyze	estimate	major
approach	evident	method
area	factor	occur
assess	finance	percent
assume	formula	period
authority	specific	principle
available	structure	proceed
benefit	theory	process
concept	vary	policy
consist	function	require
context	income	research
constitute	indicate	respond
contract	individual	role
data	interpret	section
define	involve	sector
derive	issue	significant
distribute	labor	similar
economy	legal	source
environmentestablish	legislate	

The Academic Word List
Group 2

achieve	design	potential
acquire	distinct	previous
administrate	equate	primary
affect	element	purchase
appropriate	evaluate	range
aspect	feature	region
assist	final	regulate
category	focus	relevant
chapter	impact	reside
commission	injure	resource
community	institute	restrict
complex	invest	secure
compute	item	seek
conclude	journal	select
conduct	maintain	site
consequent	normal	strategy
construct	obtain	survey
consume	participate	text
credit	perceive	tradition
culture	positive	transfer

The Academic Word List
Group 3

alternative	emphasis	physical
circumstance	ensure	proportion
comment	exclude	publish
compensate	fund	react
component	framework	register
consent	illustrate	rely
considerable	immigrate	remove
constant	imply	scheme
constrain	initial	sequence
contribute	instance	sex
convene	interact justify	shift
coordinate	layer	specify
core	link	sufficient
corporate	locate	task
correspond	maximize	technical
criteria	minor	technique
deduce	negate	technology
demonstrate	outcome	valid
document	partner	volume
dominate	philosophy	

The Academic Word List
Group 4

Access	error	parallel
adequacy	ethnic	parameter
annual	goal	phase
apparent	grant	predict
approximate	hence	prior
attitude	hypothesis	principal
attribute	implement	professional
civil	implicate	project
code	impose	promote
commit	integrate	regime
communicate	internal	resolve
concentrate	investigate	retain
confer	job	series
contrast	label	statistic
cycle	mechanism	status
debate	obvious	stress
despite	occupy	subsequent
dimension	option	sum
domestic	output	summary
emerge	overall	undertake

The Academic Word List
Group 5

academy	evolve	orient
adjust	expand	perspective
alter	expose	precise
amend	external	prime
aware	facilitate	psychology
capacity	fundamental	pursue
challenge	generate	ratio
clause	generation	reject
compound	image	revenue
conflict	liberal	stable
consult	license	style
contact	logic	substitute
decline	margin	sustain
discrete	mental	symbol
draft	medical	target
enable	modify	transit
energy	monitor	trend
enforce	network	version
entity	notion	welfare
equivalent	objective	whereas

The Academic Word List
Group 6

abstract	exceed	migrate
acknowledge	expert	minimum
accuracy	explicit	ministry
aggregate	federal	motive
allocate	fee	neutral
assign	flexible	nevertheless
attach	furthermore	overseas
author	gender	precede
bond	ignorance	presume
brief	incentive	rational
capable	incorporate	recover
cite	incidence	reveal
cooperate	index	scope
discriminate	inhibit	subsidy
display	initiate	tape
diverse	input	trace
domain	instruct	transform
edit	intelligence	transport
enhance	interval	underlie
estate	lecture	utilize

The Academic Word List
Group 7

adapt	eliminate	phenomenon
adult	empirical	priority
advocate	extract	prohibit
aid	file	publication
channel	finite	quote
chemical	foundation	release
classic	globe	reverse
comprehensive	grade	simulate
comprise	guarantee	sole
confirm	hierarchy	somewhat
contrary	identical	submit
convert	ideology	successor
couple	infer	survive
decade	innovate	thesis
definite	insert	topic
deny	intervene	transmit
differentiate	isolate	ultimate
dispose	media	unique
dynamic	mode	visible
equip	paradigm	voluntary

The Academic Word List
Group 8

abandon	deviate	plus
accompany	displace	practitioner
accumulate	drama	predominant
ambiguous	eventual	prospect
appendix	exhibit	radical
appreciate	exploit	random
arbitrary	fluctuate	reinforce
automate	guideline	restore
bias	highlight	revise
chart	implicit	schedule
clarify	induce	tense
commodity	inevitable	terminate
complement	infrastructure	theme
conform	inspect	thereby
contemporary	intense	uniform
contradict	manipulate	vehicle
crucial	minimize	via
currency	nuclear	virtual
denote	offset	visual
detect	paragraph	widespread

The Academic Word List

Group 9

accommodate	erode	protocol
analogy	ethic	qualitative
anticipate	found	refine
assure	format	relax
attain	inherent	restrain
behalf	ins insight	revolution
cease	integral	rigid
coherent	intermediate	route
coincide	manual	scenario
commence	mature	sphere
compatible	mediate	subordinate
concurrent	medium	supplement
confine	military	suspend
controversy	minimal	team
converse	mutual	temporary
device	norm	trigger
devote	overlap	unify
diminish	passive	violate
distort	portion	vision
duration	preliminary	

The Academic Word List
Group10

adjacent	odd
albeit	ongoing
assemble	panel
collapse	persist
colleague	pose
compile	reluctance
conceive	so-called
convince	straightforward
depress	undergo
encounter	whereby
enormous	
forthcoming	
incline	
integrity	
intrinsic	
invoke	
levy	
likewise	
nonetheless	
notwithstanding	

www.ingramcontent.com/pod-product-compliance
Lightning Source LLC
Chambersburg PA
CBHW051701090426
42736CB00013B/2478